OUTLINES OF VICTORIAN LITERATURE

OUTLINES OF VICTORIAN LITERATURE

BY

HUGH WALKER, LL.D.

AND

MRS HUGH WALKER

Cambridge:
at the University Press
1913

CAMBRIDGE UNIVERSITY PRESS
Cambridge, New York, Melbourne, Madrid, Cape Town,
Singapore, São Paulo, Delhi, Tokyo, Mexico City

Cambridge University Press
The Edinburgh Building, Cambridge CB2 8RU, UK

Published in the United States of America by
Cambridge University Press, New York

www.cambridge.org
Information on this title: www.cambridge.org/9781107600096

First published 1913
First paperback edition 2011

A catalogue record for this publication is available from the British Library

ISBN 978-1-107-60009-6 Paperback

PREFACE

VICTORIAN literature is a subject far too extensive and complex to be dealt with adequately in a book so short as this. The aim of the writers has been merely to furnish an introduction, to supply an outline of information and, if possible, to stimulate interest and curiosity. Their little book is based upon the larger volume by one of the writers entitled *The Literature of the Victorian Era.* The materials of that larger volume have been freely used and the same general plan has been followed. But the scale has been greatly reduced, many authors who are there discussed have been wholly omitted, and, as it may be presumed that a number of the readers will be young, care has been taken to write as simply as possible.

An attempt has been made to present the principal authors of the period not merely as writers but as men; and for this reason it will be found that the biographical element is somewhat more copious than it usually is in similar books. The purely critical element has, of course, been correspondingly curtailed. The writers have made their choice deliberately, under the conviction that the surest way to awaken the interest of beginners, and especially of such as are young in years, is to touch the note of personality.

H. W.
J. W.

LAMPETER
May 1913

CONTENTS

Chapter I. Carlyle and the Systematic Thinkers

Chapter II. Poetry

Chapter III. Novels and Novelists

CHAPTER IV. THE HISTORIANS

CHAPTER V. BIOGRAPHY AND CRITICISM

CHAPTER VI. THE FRAGMENTS THAT REMAIN

CHAPTER I

CARLYLE AND THE SYSTEMATIC THINKERS

§ 1. *Carlyle*

PEOPLE who keep pigeons have discovered that from time to time they must bring eggs from a neighbouring dovecot if they wish to keep up the excellence of their birds. If pigeon fanciers are too exclusive, and refrain from all exchange of eggs, their stock will weaken and ultimately die out. A like fate, De Quincey thinks, awaits the literature of any country which is preserved from all foreign intercourse. He says that every literature, unless it be crossed by some other of a different breed, tends to superannuation; and he points to the French as an example of one which has suffered, so as to be, in his opinion, on the point of extinction, because it has rejected all alliance with exotic literature. Writing nearly a century ago, in 1821, he asks what, with this example before our eyes, the English should do, and answers, "Evidently we should cultivate an intercourse with that literature of Europe which has most of a juvenile constitution." "That," he adds, "is the German literature." What De Quincey recommended has been done, and the Victorian era may be described as the era of German Influence.

Sir Walter Scott and Coleridge were among the first great men to find their way into German literature; but its best interpreter has been Thomas Carlyle (1795—1881); and for this reason, not less than because of his date and his intrinsic importance, his name is naturally the first to be introduced into a study of Victorian Literature. No one else touches it at so many points; no one else combines in the same degree the vital principles of poetry and prose; no one else did so much to make the literature of his age what it became.

In his relation to Germany Carlyle's importance is very great. He laboured to understand her philosophy and to do justice to her spirit. The greatest of German poets, Goethe, was his hero, and the idealism which the German philosophers preached became, we might almost say, his religion. Carlyle learnt from German thinkers to understand himself and to find expression for the new thoughts which he brought into English literature. "Germanism" is the master key to much of the English literature of the nineteenth century; and it was Carlyle who naturalised German thought in England.

Carlyle was born in the little Scottish border village of Ecclefechan. His father was a stonemason and his mother a peasant woman who, late in life, taught herself to write in order that she might answer the letters of her famous son. There was no money to spare in this workman's cottage, but thrifty habits and simple food left a narrow margin of the weekly earnings for the education of the children. The deep religious convictions of the parents prompted them to make many sacrifices so that they might prepare one son for the ministry. With this end in view Thomas Carlyle attended the academy at Annan, and walked six miles each morning to school and six miles back again at night.

At the Annan Academy the famous preacher Edward Irving had been a pupil, but it was not till Carlyle had left Annan that the two youths met. They were each destined subsequently to exercise much influence on the other's life. After his university career Irving taught at Haddington and later at Kirkcaldy. Meanwhile Carlyle had entered the University of Edinburgh, to which he refers in *Sartor Resartus* as "the worst of all hitherto discovered universities." The true university of these days, he declared, was a collection of books; and so it certainly was in his case. He quickly discovered that he was suited neither to the life of a student in a theological college, nor to the life of a parish minister for which it was the preparation. There remained only the work of teaching open to him; so he followed Edward Irving to Kirkcaldy and taught another school there. The acquaintance of the two Annan men rapidly developed into a close intimacy; and when, one vacation, Irving took his friend with him to visit the home of Dr Welsh of Haddington, Carlyle met Dr Welsh's only child, Jane, his future wife. She had previously been taught by Irving, and between pupil and master there was a warm affection, which might have ripened into love had Carlyle not been introduced. Jane Welsh was at this time very attractive and gifted with wit that almost equalled Carlyle's own in sharpness and cleverness. In 1826 they were married, and began life in a small home at Comely Bank near Edinburgh. Froude has told the story of their life together, and has left the world with the impression that they were both unhappy. The word happiness requires interpretation. If it means leading from day to day a contented existence of unruffled calm, then the Carlyles were not happy. But the fault lay in their temperaments, not in their affection. They were both persons of genius, and had in an unusual degree the gift of picturesque and humorous language. They enjoyed using their powers on each other, and the domestic explosions meant little more to them than capering and rearing mean to a high-spirited horse. It is true they sometimes damaged themselves, just as the horse does too; but, like him also, they were ready again to take the bit between their teeth at the next opportunity. Froude, who was ill-endowed with a sense of humour, took everything they said seriously, and marked down tragedy when the actors were playing burlesque.

Except for these tea-cup storms the life of Carlyle was uneventful. Its chief milestones are the beginning and ending of his books. It was the books which settled for him his place of residence. Two years after his marriage, to secure himself the leisure and the freedom from interruption which were necessary for writing, he moved from Edinburgh to Craigenputtock, a lonely farm-house on the Galloway hills, the property of his wife. There Carlyle lived for six years, which proved to be the intellectual seed time of his life. His *Life of Schiller* and the translation of Goethe's *Wilhelm Meister's Apprenticeship* were written before his removal thither. It was during his residence at Craigenputtock that Goethe and he exchanged letters and gifts, and that Emerson crossed the Atlantic and came to pay him homage. *Sartor Resartus*, or "the tailor patched," was the chief work of this period; but he wrote besides essays on Burns, Voltaire, Diderot, Johnson and Novalis, the second essay on Richter, *The Diamond Necklace* and *Signs of the Times*.

Nichol in his life of Carlyle says that his work "marks the beginning of a new era in the history of British criticism." There is exaggeration in this judgment, but there is also some truth. Carlyle has taught us that there can be no justice in criticism which is not based on sympathy with the work reviewed. "No man," he says, "can pronounce dogmatically, with even a chance of being right, on the faults of a poem, till he has seen its very best and highest beauty;...the beauty of the poem as a whole in the strict sense; the clear view of it as an indivisible unity."

And this could only be done by viewing it from the author's standpoint. It was in this spirit that Carlyle prepared himself for his task of literary critic, biographer, or historian. It is interesting to notice that Carlyle did his work well exactly in proportion to his fidelity in following the laws which he had himself laid down. A poem and the life of a great man are, in Carlyle's view, closely related to each other. "There is no heroic poem," he says, "in the world but is at bottom a biography, the life of a man"; and conversely "there is no life of a man, faithfully recorded, but is a heroic poem of its sort, rhymed or unrhymed." In all Carlyle's works there is no idea so deep rooted, or so variously expressed, as that of the supreme importance of the great man. To discover him and then to do him and his works justice, Carlyle regards as the first duty of every writer of criticism and history. This is the essence of his book on *Heroes and Hero-Worship*, and it is constantly repeated in *Past and Present* and in *Latter-Day Pamphlets*. His *Cromwell* and *Frederick the Great* are further examples of the same doctrine, and even his *French Revolution* itself is made, not always easily, to revolve round individuals, and above all round the person of Mirabeau. In *Sartor Resartus* Carlyle writes that "Great men are the inspired Texts of that divine Book of Revelations, whereof a chapter is completed from epoch to epoch, and by some named History."

The last-named book was a puzzle to Carlyle's own critics. He went up to London in 1831 to arrange for its publication. The MS was offered to John Murray, the best-known publisher of his time. He accepted *Sartor*, and then changed his mind. The book finally started its career in the pages of *Fraser's Magazine*, and justified the refusal of Murray by proving to be "beyond measure unpopular" with the readers of that journal. Taine, the French critic, writes of its author in much the same terms as the readers of *Fraser* spoke of his book. Taine calls Carlyle "a strange animal, a relic of a lost family, a sort of Mastodon, who has strayed in a world not made for him."

It is small wonder that this "strange animal," author of a book still stranger, failed to earn a living wage. In 1834, when the Carlyles removed to Cheyne Row, Chelsea, the available money with which they had to face their new life was £200. In the following year Carlyle wrote, "it is now some three-and-twenty months since I have earned one penny by the craft of literature." This was the position at thirty-nine of the greatest literary genius of the age, while the commonplace Martin Tupper was able, a decade later, to make from £500 to £800 a year by his stale *Proverbial Philosophy*. The outlook for Carlyle was dark and gloomy. He had no prospect of earning except by his writings, and his latest and greatest work was threatening to bring ruin upon the magazine which had given it a home. The knowledge that *Sartor Resartus* had appeared in book form in America before it came out thus in England inclined its author to consider the idea of trying his fortunes there. Emerson had assured him that he could by lecturing make an income sufficient for his needs. He would probably have emigrated. But Harriet Martineau and several others determined to make an effort to keep him in England; and the outcome was a series of six lectures on German literature, delivered in 1837. The work was odious to Carlyle, but it was completely successful, and the £135 it brought in cleared away the money difficulties that had encompassed him. In each of the three following years he gave a fresh set of lectures, the last being the famous series on heroes.

Carlyle neither spoke nor wrote with ease. When he arrived to settle in London his mind was full of the history he proposed to write of *The French Revolution*. Yet in his journal he records that "after two weeks of blotching and bloring" he has managed to produce—"two clean pages" of the book. Nevertheless, in this work we find some of the best examples of the vivid picturesqueness of Carlyle's descriptions. He accurately described his method of work when he declared his intention "to splash down what he knew in large masses of colour, that it may look like a smoke-and-flame conflagration in the distance." When the last sentence of *The French Revolution* was written Carlyle went out for a walk, saying to his wife, "I know not whether this book is worth anything, nor what the world will do with it, or misdo, or entirely forbear to do, as is likeliest; but this I could tell the world: You have not had for a hundred years any book that comes more direct and flamingly from the heart of a living man." *The French Revolution* received recognition at once, and its author took his place henceforth as one of the foremost English men of letters. It was in connexion with this book that an accident occurred which gave evidence of Carlyle's amazing courage and self-control in great trials. The MS of the first volume was lent to his friend John Stuart Mill to read. While in his custody the precious pages were used by a careless housemaid as fire-lighters; yet when told of the catastrophe Carlyle made no reproaches, but set himself to re-write it, and finished it just a year after he began the composition of the version which had been destroyed.

There was no lack of moral force in Carlyle, and no man ever attracted him unless he was strong. His two heroes, Cromwell and Frederick, seem to stand out in opposition to each other; but in his mind they represented the same ideal—the moving power of great men, and their certain triumph. Sir Henry Taylor in his autobiography remarks on the strangeness of what he believes to be the fact that such a man as Carlyle should have chosen success as the object of his idolatry, and tells an amusing story in illustration. "Long before his life of Cromwell came out, I heard him insisting in conversation on the fact that Cromwell had been invariably successful; and having with much satisfaction traced the long line of his successes to the end, he added, 'it is true they got him out of his grave at the Restoration and they stuck his head up over the gate at Tyburn, but not till he had quite done with it.'" This story is characteristic of Carlyle, but Taylor has misunderstood it. Mere success was contemptible to the author of the essay on Burns; what he set store upon was that power of which success was usually the index.

In his *Cromwell* and *Frederick the Great* Carlyle was at his best. The first was suggested to him by Mill, who asked him for an article upon the Protector for *The London and Westminster Review.* Carlyle agreed to do it; but in the interval Mill went abroad and his sub-editor informed Carlyle that he "meant to do Cromwell himself." In rage Carlyle determined to lengthen the article into a book. It was the research work necessary for his task that roused him to set on foot the London Library. He intended to write a life of Cromwell and a history of the Commonwealth, but what he ultimately produced was an inspired piece of editorial work on Cromwell's letters and speeches combined with a magnificent picture of the Captain of the Ironsides, and vivid descriptions of the battle of Dunbar and other scenes in which he is the leading figure.

A couple of years before *Cromwell* was published Carlyle achieved what, to him, was a miracle: he wrote *Past and Present* in seven weeks and uttered not a single groan during its production. It, and its predecessor, *Chartism*, and its successor, *Latter-Day Pamphlets*, form a trio of books inspired by the social condition of England in his time. They are filled with a radical's hatred of class tyranny, yet at the same time they show the profoundest respect for the *principle* of aristocracy.

The *Life of Sterling*, like *Past and Present*, was written quickly and easily. It is a beautiful life of a beautiful character, and stands out in its language in marked contrast to the rugged though eloquent style of Carlyle's other compositions. After *Sterling* came *The History of Frederick II of Prussia, called Frederick the Great* (1858—1865), the last important work of Carlyle. It was by far the longest of his books, and the most difficult to write. After its completion he wrote: "If they were to offer me all Prussia, all the solar system, I would not write *Frederick* again." He set about his task with characteristic thoroughness, visiting Germany to gather materials and to study the scenes of Frederick's battles. Without this careful attention to detail many of his pictures would have been wanting in vividness and in accuracy. Thanks to it, his work remained, in the opinion of Germans, the best general history of Frederick and the most reliable picture of his campaigns until the eighties, when fuller knowledge was obtained by the opening of the German archives, and the publication of the correspondence of Frederick.

Carlyle's profound belief in strength, as symbolised for him by men like Cromwell and Frederick, has alienated many. They do not see that the terms "might" and "right," in his use of them, are interchangeable. If we give them centuries to try it in, Carlyle holds that we may say indifferently "might is right" or "right is might." The universe is just, and, in the long run, right is bound to triumph. But the triumph must be won by effort. Carlyle kept always before his eyes the need of fighting for justice and truth. These were the chief articles of his faith. No one ever preached his creed more persistently; and, what is more difficult, no one ever lived more consistently in accordance with his creed. Neither by word, nor by action, nor by refraining from action, would he palter with what seemed to him to be the truth. For this lesson alone, if for nothing else, the world would have cause to rank him among its great men. But in spite of his almost fanatical worship of truth, Carlyle's fantastic humour and his command of language occasionally, as the phrase goes, made his tongue or his pen run away with him and caused him to make the most glaring misrepresentations and exaggerations. Cardinal Newman had not, in his estimation, "the intellect of a moderate-sized rabbit"; John Stuart Mill, the philosopher, was "a man of aridities and negations"; and Scott was "the restaurateur of Europe." So too the great civil war between North and South in America, which swept off the population of a small state, was to Carlyle "a smoky chimney which had taken fire." Yet this power of phrase-making is among the greatest of literary gifts, and made him, with his humour, the most brilliant talker of his day. His most distinguished contemporaries listened enthralled by his eloquence and by his originality. The servants who waited at tables where he dined ran from the room choking down their laughter at his bursts of humour. His phrases could cut like a surgeon's knife, or dazzle like a reflected sunbeam, or bring before the eye in a dozen words a portrait never to be forgotten. Thus Tennyson is "a fine, large-featured, dim-eyed, bronze-coloured, shaggy-headed man,...dusty, smoky, free and easy," and Mazzini, the famous Italian refugee and patriot, "a small, square-headed, bright-eyed, swift, yet still Ligurian figure; beautiful and merciful and fierce."

Carlyle lived a long life and his recognition came in good time. Perhaps the hour of highest triumph to him was his election to the Lord Rectorship of his old university of Edinburgh. This great hour held also the moment of his deepest agony, for as he turned away from the speeches and pageants of the Edinburgh ceremony he learnt that his wife had been found dead in her carriage driving home to Chelsea from the Park. Her death was due to a paroxysm of horror at seeing her little dog, as she supposed, crushed under a passing wheel. The animal escaped unhurt, but the human heart ceased to beat. With her life Carlyle's own practically ended. He survived her for many years, but he was for the most part condemned to idleness. His hand trembled so that he could not write, and he found it impossible to dictate his thoughts to another. He died, as he had long lived, in Cheyne Row, but he was buried amongst his kinsfolk in the kirkyard of Ecclefechan, just behind the cottage in which he was born.

§ 2. *The Theologians*

It may seem at first sight superfluous to devote a section in a small history of literature to the work of theologians. But in the Victorian era the religious movements had an indirect influence upon men of letters quite out of proportion to the literary value of the work their exponents produced. In Scotland the Disruption profoundly influenced the whole life of the nation, while in England the theologians of the Oxford Movement gave a different colour to the minds of certain poets and painters, from whom we have had verses and paintings which would have been very different but for this theological influence.

In England the Catholic reaction was full of literary significance, for it was really one of the forms in which the great romance movement expressed itself. Scott in his novels had turned men's minds back to the middle ages and had awakened interest in all their mystery and mysticism. Cardinal Newman says that the Waverley romances created in him a Catholic frame of mind, and the staunch Protestant George Borrow confirms the view of the Catholic Newman, by denouncing Scott for reviving men's interest in Jacobitism and Popery.

There was, then, religious unrest and dissatisfaction North and South of the Tweed. In Scotland a large section of the Presbyterian body regarded the existing system of patronage as incompatible with the highest spiritual life; and ultimately these high-minded enthusiasts decided to leave their national church rather than submit longer to this wrong. In 1843, therefore, about 450 ministers with their followers marched into the wilderness with a Bible in one hand and a Confession of Faith in the other. The leader of this bold movement was Thomas Chalmers (1780—1847), and upon him fell the responsibliity of finding means of support for the men who had left their manses and given up their endowments to follow him. To meet their needs Chalmers created the famous Sustentation Fund of the Free Kirk—that is, his was the organising brain behind it. His plan was the very genius of simplicity. By a simple arithmetical calculation he showed that a contribution of one penny a week from each member of the seceding Kirk would provide a stipend of £150 a year for each minister. The iron was hot and he struck. From the first the people recognised that if they would have spiritual independence they must pay for it. And they paid. Chalmers had already in his parish of St John's, Glasgow, given proof of his unusual gifts of statesmanship in his administration of poor relief. He lived there during a period of industrial revolution, when men were thrown out of work by the introduction of machinery. The recent wars in Europe had raised the price of food, and when Chalmers entered his parish he found that the annual money devoted to the relief of the poor was £1400. In three years he reduced this to £280, and at the same time raised the poor by his administration and teaching to a condition of greater comfort.

The advent of the Free Kirk of Scotland and the history of poor relief in Glasgow are not literature, yet it has seemed worth while to touch briefly upon the work of Chalmers because his social activity had a far-reaching though indirect influence upon the intelligence of his generation. He deserves to be remembered for the things he did, rather than for the books he wrote, though his contemporary fame as an author was so great that his *Discourses on the Christian Revelation*, which appeared at the same time as *Old Mortality* by Sir Walter Scott, sold as rapidly as the popular novel. In the history of Chalmers, also, we are again brought into touch with Carlyle, for his early friend Edward Irving (1792—1834) was Chalmers's assistant in Glasgow. The natural gifts of Irving were great, but there was probably a want of balance in his mind; for in spite of the high hopes of men such as Carlyle, Chalmers and the historian Thirlwall, Irving squandered his powers in spiritual excesses, and believed that he and his people would see the end of the world and the inauguration of Christ in an earthly kingdom. Carlyle listened grimly to the famous "tongues" in Irving's church, and described them as a "shrieky hysterical lall-lall-lall"; while Mrs Carlyle sardonically remarked that had she married Irving they would not have been heard.

South of the Tweed men did not concern themselves with patronage, but with the broad doctrines taught in the pulpits and the indifferent administration of the services and sacraments of the Church of England. German philosophy had found its way among the theologians and disturbed their minds, and the discoveries of scientific thinkers had troubled the still waters of orthodoxy. Men zealous for the safety of their beliefs dared not look forward; it seemed to them wiser to turn backward and seek shelter under the authority of a church which claims to be infallible. To some of them it did not appear impossible to put the ecclesiastical clock back three hundred years. Separate from, but side by side with, these enthusiasts were another group of churchmen who joined forces with them only because the renewal of mediæval ritual pleased their sense of decorum and beauty, and remedied the irreverence and carelessness which had crept into the administration of the services. Behind both parties was the impelling force of the romance writers, driving men back from materialism into the age of mystery and miracle.

Among such men was John Henry Newman (1801—1890), who was educated at Trinity College, Oxford, and became Fellow of Oriel in 1822. He describes himself as superstitious in his youth, and as finding comfort in childhood in crossing himself after the fashion of Roman Catholics when he went into the dark. He ultimately joined that body to which apparently his earliest feelings had drawn him; but it was ten years before he found where his mind was leading him. His first publication was *Lives of the English Saints*. In this work he was helped by his followers. Next came a series of papers entitled *Tracts for the Times*. Newman wrote twenty-nine of these, and the most Romish of all, Tract XC, was from his pen. *The Development of Christian Doctrine*, and two very disappointing novels, *Loss and Gain*, and *Callista*, came after he had left the Church of England for that of Rome. The stories were written to attract men to follow him thither. Newman also wrote poetry, his most notable pieces being the exquisite *Dream of Gerontius*, and the beautiful hymn *Lead, kindly Light*. The *Apologia pro Vita Sua*, his greatest contribution to literature, was written from the Oratory, Birmingham, where he finished his life. It is the record of the spiritual experiences which led him to Rome. It reveals the anxious fears and eager hopes with which he was consumed before he left the Church of England.

Newman was the literary genius of the Oxford Movement, as this religious revival is called. Froude said he was the indicating number, all the rest being but as ciphers in comparison. Oxford was the home not only of this movement, but also of the Noetics, the school of theologians who sought to harmonise their religious beliefs with their reasoning faculties. Fear and distrust of this school profoundly influenced Newman and his friends, and Tract XC was more than this Protestant section of the community, for its part, could endure. There was a tremendous commotion, and Newman was driven from his fellowship at Oriel College and from his position as tutor. He retired to Littlemore, near by, and gathered round him such of the Tractarians as were disposed to go as far as he then did; for he still hesitated before taking the final step and seceding from the Anglican Communion.

No one has ever surpassed Newman in the delicate charm of his English. Refinement, severity, strength, sweetness—all these are attributes of his style, as well as of his character. There was no one in the movement comparable to him, but there are a few minor writers who deserve to be mentioned. Newman says that the Oxford revival was started in 1833, by a sermon on *National Apostasy* preached by his friend John Keble (1792—1866) at the opening of the Oxford assizes. But though the conflagration was great it does not follow that there was greatness in the spark which started it. The real work was done by Newman; and Keble's place in literature must depend upon *The Christian Year*, a volume of religious poetry, concerning which a famous Cambridge divine declared that one verse of it was worth volumes of Tennyson. Such a criticism only leads us to "disable the judgment" of the critic. There is far more insight in Bagehot's saying that Keble had translated Wordsworth into the language of women.

Among the Tractarians who remained, like Keble, in the Church of England, the most influential, and in some ways the greatest, was Edward Bouverie Pusey (1800—1882). So conspicuous was he that the section of the party to which he belonged came to be widely known by his name:

they were the Puseyites. He was a man of profound learning, and, unlike Newman, he was familiar with German philosophy. But he shrank from its conclusions, and apparently, in later days, even regretted his own early studies in it.

The Oxford revivalists dreaded the rationalism which German philosophy seemed to foster, and distrusted its influence upon their students. They thought they saw the evil they dreaded exemplified in their own country and their own university. Richard Whately, afterwards Archbishop of Dublin, and Thomas Arnold, the famous father of a famous son, were among the Noetics mentioned above; and their "liberal" theology was the ever-present dread of Newman. The influence in after days of the boys trained by Arnold at Rugby showed that Newman had, from his own point of view, good ground for his fears. Akin in spirit to these men was Connop Thirlwall, the first theologian to study German theology seriously. He translated Schleiermacher's *Critical Essay on Luke.* It is somewhat surprising to find him afterwards amongst the orthodox clergy who condemned the writers of *Essays and Reviews* and took proceedings against them.

Among the Oxford theologians who followed Thirlwall's lead and studied German literature and philosophy were Benjamin Jowett (1817—1893) and his friend Arthur Penrhyn Stanley (1815—1881), afterwards Dean of Westminster. They made a tour of Germany together and brought back ideas which were afterwards to startle Oxford. Jowett's first exposition of these ideas appeared in an essay on *Interpretation* contributed to the celebrated *Essays and Reviews,* a volume of papers from different writers which caused an uproar among the High Church party, almost equal to the disturbance which Newman's Tract XC had awakened in the hearts of the Low Churchmen. Two of the seven contributors were prosecuted, and Jowett was excluded for many years from preaching outside the walls of Balliol College. After this criticism he turned from theology and set about the *Translation of Plato*, which is his most valuable contribution to literature.

The history of the extraordinarily influential movement in which these writers and many others were diversely interested is best read in Newman's *Apologia*, which, although only a spiritual autobiography, throws more light on the religious history of that period than anything else that has been written. *The Oxford Movement* by Richard William Church (1815—1889) ranks second to Newman's great work—a distant second. Church was one of the most accomplished literary critics as well as one of the foremost ecclesiastics of his time. But accomplished as he was, Church was the incarnation of modesty. It has been said of him that he is the only author who has ever written the history of events in which he took a large part without mentioning his own name.

These men belong to literature, as we said before, not so much because of what they wrote, as because the movement of which they formed part, though it produced few notable books, influenced many minds, and left its traces on things so diverse as poetry, architecture, painting, and even furniture and wall-papers. The Pre-Raphaelites were not Newmanites, but they would have been different men had it not been for Newman's work.

§ 3. *The Philosophers*

For purposes of clearness the philosophers of the Victorian era may be divided into the men of the Scottish School, the Utilitarians, the Positivists and the English Hegelians. The students of the philosophy of history form a group apart.

The Scottish professor of philosophy has a position of

very great power, if only he knows how to use it. Year after year scores of young men, on the whole the *élite* of the country, pass under his influence. They are nearly all more or less imbued with the national taste for speculation, nearly all disposed to regard the professor as an oracle. They become in after life, each in his own sphere, the leaders of the nation. The advocate at the bar, the village minister, doctor, lawyer, schoolmaster, thus receive their education ; and through them the influence of one powerful mind may filter down to hundreds and thousands who never heard so much as the name of the teacher. Ever since the revival of the Scottish universities in the eighteenth century there have been a few men who have known how to wield this influence. Sir William Hamilton (1788—1856), professor of logic and metaphysics in Edinburgh University, was one of them. Until his appointment to this position philosophy had somewhat lost ground. Professor Campbell Fraser declares that in 1836, the year of Hamilton's appointment, it was at a lower ebb than it had ever been in Scotland since the coming of Francis Hutcheson from Ireland. It fell to Hamilton to lift it once more to its old position.

Hamilton had reached middle life when he took up his work in Edinburgh. He had the advantage of the training of both a Scottish and an English university. He studied for the bar, and acquired sufficient legal skill to establish his own claim to a baronetcy. But his first interest was philosophy. He read enormously, and scarcely any subject came amiss. Even witchcraft commended itself to him for serious study. Unfortunately there is little fruit of this industry. His work was mainly done in the lecture rooms, and his chief contribution to philosophy, *Lectures on Metaphysics and Logic*, was not published until after his death. Hamilton's value as a philosopher was seriously diminished by his devotion to the teaching of his Scottish predecessors, and by his inability or unwillingness to recognise the importance of the principles to be found in the works of the German philosopher Kant. The St Andrews philosopher Ferrier says that Hamilton would have done better "had he built entirely on his own foundation, instead of trying to defend a worn-out system against the attacks of the sceptic philosopher Hume." Ferrier believed that Hamilton had it in him, had he worked independently, to build up theories which were likely to endure.

It was left to Hamilton's pupil, Henry Longueville Mansel (1820—1871), Dean of St Paul's, to adapt the teaching of his master to theology. His most original book is his *Limits of Religious Thought*. It attracted much attention, and provoked intense dislike in the minds of Maurice, Mill, and Huxley. The last named compared Mansel to the drunken fellow in the picture of a contested election by Hogarth, who is sawing through a signpost on the outer end of which he is sitting. Huxley meant that the signpost was Church doctrine, the doctrine held in St Paul's, and Mansel, the Dean, was unconsciously cutting it in two.

The sway of the Scottish philosophers ended with the first half of the nineteenth century, and their place was taken in the third quarter by the Utilitarians. The founder of this school was Jeremy Bentham, and his prophet was James Mill, the father of J. S. Mill. Their formula was "the greatest happiness of the greatest number," and they taught that this happiness depended mainly on material conditions and was identical with pleasure.

With the exception of John Stuart Mill (1806—1873), the son of James Mill, the Utilitarians have contributed little to literature; but we owe to their initiative some of our greatest social reforms. They were the pioneers of free education; they fought for that liberty of thought which, besides conferring other benefits, has flung open the learning of Oxford and Cambridge to dissenters; and they were the champions of the democracy whose advent to power is the greatest political feature of this country and of the nineteenth century. As their greatest man is J. S. Mill it is of interest to examine the atmosphere in which he was brought up. His father educated him. He allowed the boy to read neither poetry nor romance, and shut him out from all the influences of religion. Everything tended to repression so strongly that it has even been suggested that the real John Stuart Mill may never have lived. As a boy, he was a prodigy in learning. At three years of age, a mere baby in the nursery, he learnt Greek. When he grew to manhood he found himself, he says, "with an advantage of a quarter of a century over my contemporaries"; and when we find men of talent, and even of genius, who were ten or twelve years his seniors, treating him even in boyhood as an equal, we see that there must have been good ground for the assertion.

This early recognition of his great gifts neither produced conceit nor diminished the simple beauty of Mill's character. Sir Henry Taylor declared him to be so naturally and necessarily good that men hardly thought of him as having occasion for a conscience. Gladstone called him the "saint of rationalism," and the painter Watts's portrait of him, fascinating in its delicate refinement, justifies this description. The secret of this attractiveness may be found in the simple rule of life which he set before himself: "Try thyself unweariedly till thou findest the highest thing thou art capable of doing, faculties and outward circumstance being both duly considered, and then DO IT."

Mill married the widow of a certain Mr Taylor. She seems to have been a woman of unusual powers; at any rate he attributes all his highest work to her inspiration. It may be that her sympathetic comprehension of his nature helped him to break down the self-repression due to his early training, and increased his enjoyment of life and his powers of production. In his generosity he laid at her feet honours that were his own. For thirty years Mill lived a strenuous life. He worked as civil servant in the India Office, and did his literary work after this daily toil was over. He was elected Member of Parliament for Westminster, having been chosen, as candidates rarely are, for his distinction in philosophy and his interest in good government. At the election of 1868, however, this constituency forgot its high ideals, and Mill was defeated. A few years later he retired to Avignon, where he died.

The *System of Logic* is Mill's most original work. It has been superseded now, but for a time it was the text book on its subject, and it was one of the most influential books of the nineteenth century. Bagehot, the economist, said, when Mill died, that half the minds of the younger generation of Englishmen had been coloured by the *Logic*. *The Principles of Political Economy* is less original than the *Logic*, but it is interesting, because in it Mill finds place for his views upon government, land tenure, rent and other economic problems. The little book upon *Liberty* would also deserve notice, were it only because the writer is so profoundly in earnest. Nothing roused Mill to fiercer wrath than an infringement of liberty, whether it was in the name of the sovereign, or of the mob, or of religion, or of law. In another sense also this book is important. Although it was published in the same year as Darwin's *Origin of Species*, it is remarkable, as are all the works of the Utilitarians, for the total absence of any recognition in it of the idea of heredity. Hegel and Herbert Spencer in philosophy, and Lamarck, Lyell and Darwin in science, all live and breathe in the atmosphere created by the idea of evolution. It is the master thought of the century; yet not only Mill but all the Utilitarians write as if it did not exist.

Among the names of those who in later days have partially followed Mill, there is none more honoured or more honourable than that of Henry Sidgwick (1838–1900). He began work in Cambridge as a classical lecturer, but discovered that his true interest lay in moral science. He exchanged his classical post for a lectureship in moral philosophy at a time when this school was in its infancy. More than twenty years later he became professor of the subject in Cambridge. His three important works are *Methods of Ethics*, *Principles of Political Economy* and *Elements of Politics*. The names of two of them suggest that application of philosophy to the difficulties of ordinary life which marks the work of Mill.

The next philosophical group, the Positivists, contains four names of special interest—George Eliot, George Henry Lewes, Harriet Martineau and Richard Congreve, the last of whom founded the Positivist community in London. The founder of Positivism was the French thinker, Comte. He had the vice, rare in French writers, of obscurity. His manner of expressing himself was so confusing, even in his own language, that the paraphrase made by Harriet Martineau of his works was translated into French and became one of the chief channels through which his fellow-countrymen learnt to understand his ideas. These had a great attraction for persons like Harriet Martineau and George Eliot, who felt their religious beliefs crumbling in the conflict between reason and faith. They thought that they had found in their love for Humanity an object of worship which could satisfy the soul without offending the intellect.

In the novels of George Eliot positivism was merely one of many strains of thought, and as a system it is only of secondary importance in her work. But G. H. Lewes (1817–1878), afterwards her husband, expounded it in his books, *Comte's Philosophy of the Sciences*, and *Problems of Life and*

Mind. In the *History of Philosophy* too he shows himself an ardent disciple. But the versatility of Lewes's genius and the variety of his attainments made his work bright and attractive rather than profound, and left his readers suspicious that in his philosophical works he had furnished them with "the art of amusing themselves with method," rather than with a reason for their faith. Thackeray expressed the contemporary feeling entertained for Lewes when he declared that he would not be surprised to see him riding down Piccadilly on a white elephant.

There was none of Lewes's light-heartedness in the philosophy of Harriet Martineau (1802—1876). She came of a Unitarian family and was brought up in that intellectual society which, with the even more famous artistic set, found a home in Norwich in the beginning of the century. In disposition she was somewhat like the dog which Dr John Brown describes as unable to get his fill of fighting. "Dogmatic, hasty, imperious," W. R. Greg calls her. She was a woman more likely to influence by the force of her writings than by their charm. Yet she wrote a novel, *Deerbrook,* which Caroline Fox says "inspires trust and love, faith in its fulness, resignation in its meekness." She wrote histories, tales illustrative of the laws of political economy, and many pamphlets on questions of government. But the book by which her fame will live is her *Positive Philosophy of Auguste Comte,* in which she not merely condenses but interprets the philosopher's meaning.

The Hegelian was another school of philosophy of foreign extraction which was destined to spread its influence far and wide in England. The Germans have given us in the principles of Hegel and, in the more distant past, of Kant, a point of view which has influenced the whole of our thought. These new ideals filtered into the English mind through the writings of Coleridge and Carlyle; but they were not, until a more recent date, embodied in formal works on the subject. The first home of the English Hegelians was in Oxford, and Jowett, the Master of Balliol, already mentioned amongst the theologians, was the most influential of the school. Although he would have objected to being called a Hegelian, it is the spirit of this philosophy which arrests and interests us in his commentaries on the Thessalonians, Galatians and Romans, and also in his introductions to Plato. Writing of Hegelianism, Jowett says, "It is impossible to be satisfied with any other system, after you have begun with this." It was under his care that this school of thought was nourished, and it is in the works of his pupils, T. H. Green and Edward Caird, that the younger generation of thinkers have found the system formulated for their study. Jowett contributed nothing to the expansion of the system. Perhaps his greatest legacy to his country has been his high conception of the ends and aims of University life. He was not oblivious of the value of high scholarship, but he laid much greater stress upon the training of the undergraduates for work in life and for the service of their fellow men. Among the men whom he moulded was the philosopher Thomas Hill Green (1836—1882), whose greatest work, the *Prolegomena to Ethics*, was published after the death of its author. Green is one of the deepest thinkers of the century. He sets himself the task of refuting the Utilitarian idea that to attain pleasure or happiness is the true end of an action. The object of man's struggle on earth ought to be, Green feels, "some perfection of human life, some realization of human life." It should be sufficient for mankind to know that there is an improvement in conduct and character, and it should not be necessary that this improvement should be accompanied by increased pleasure.

Green's writings are very hard to follow because of his inability to express himself easily and simply, and his contemporary Edward Caird (1835—1908) has for this reason, and also because of his longer life, been able to do greater work than he as a teacher and writer upon Hegelianism. The methods of the two men were singularly different. Green sought to make his meaning clear to the student, by finding in some other philosopher, like Hume, whom he happened to be criticising, a thought in opposition to his own. Caird, on the other hand, found it more helpful to search for points of agreement between himself and the writer he was explaining. Caird held the professorship of moral philosophy in Glasgow University for twenty-seven years. When he succeeded to it his subject had fallen into disrepute; when he left in 1893 to succeed Jowett as Master of Balliol, he had won for himself and for his school of philosophy the respect of all scholars, and was recognised as the greatest of all living exponents of Hegelianism. Caird was eminently fair minded. He made no converts by violence, but probably no man who understood his lectures failed to be permanently influenced by him. His best known books are *The Evolution of Religion* and *The Evolution of Theology in the Greek Philosophers.* His treatise on *The Critical Philosophy of Kant* is more technical, and therefore to most readers more difficult than the others.

James Martineau (1805—1900), the gifted brother of Harriet Martineau, though he differed from Caird and Green in principle and method, was like them in his appreciation of German philosophy. With his name may be coupled that of F. W. Newman (1805—1897), the learned brother of Cardinal Newman, who had travelled far on the path of scepticism while his brother was moving towards Rome. Martineau became professor of mental and moral philosophy at Manchester New College, Oxford, and F. W. Newman held a post on the same teaching staff. *Phases of Faith*, by Newman, is a sincere and readable account of his own spiritual experiences, but his book *The Soul*, so popular at its publication, is now hardly remembered. Martineau has written books which place him high among the philosophers of the time. And he has a claim for remembrance in his high-mindedness, and in the simple integrity of his life. His principal books are *Studies of Christianity*, *A Study of Spinoza*, *Types of Ethical Theory* and *The Seat of Authority in Religion.*

Side by side with these French and German schools of philosophy was the English school of evolution; but its pioneer, Charles Darwin, was a man of science and its history comes later, in the section devoted to science.

There remain three men of great interest in connexion with the philosophy of history—Buckle, Maine, and Bagehot. They are taken together because of their endeavour, in their various books, to study history from a philosophical standpoint. They have tried, not to give a narrative of past events, but to abstract from the history of the events related by others a body of principles and laws.

Henry Thomas Buckle (1821—1862) was a delicate child, and home tuition had often to supplement the regular work of school, which he left at fourteen. He did not go to a University, and this may account for some of the deficiencies and also for much of the freshness of his work. He read everything he could lay hands upon, and had a memory which rivalled that of Macaulay in its tenacity. The result was that at twenty-nine he found himself with a working knowledge of nineteen languages. The death of his father eight years before had left him in possession, like Darwin, of a sufficient fortune; and thus he was enabled to follow the bent of his own mind. Buckle believed that the movements of men, which appear to be controlled by their own caprice, or shall we say will, are really governed by laws. On the surface a man appears to marry when he will, to select his own business or profession according to his own inclination, to go abroad or stay at home as fancy dictates. An examination of statistics suggests that all these voluntary acts are really done in obedience to laws. If food is costly the number of marriages decreases; if there is a demand for schoolmasters the training colleges are full and more lecturers are required; if labour is needed abroad the wages in that locality go up and emigrants flock thither. The task of the philosopher of history is to discover the tables of stone on which these laws are written. He has no early records to search; he must work backward from the event to its cause. Buckle, referring to his own labours, says, "I have been long convinced, that the progress of every people is regulated by principles—or, as they are called, laws—as regular and certain as those which govern the physical world. To discover those laws is the object of my work." In speaking of his *History of Civilization in England* he says, "It is an attempt to rescue history from the hands of annalists, chroniclers and antiquarians." The plan of this book was formed in early life, and Buckle gave up the whole of his manhood to it. The first volume placed him high in the rank of men of letters, and the second was equally popular. The third appeared after his death. Contemporary with it there appeared Carlyle's volumes on *Frederick the Great*, and it is suggestive to compare the different points of view of these two writers. Buckle expected to find among average men the key to their own age; Carlyle, on the other hand, insisted that it can only be found in the thoughts of the greatest.

Sir Henry Sumner Maine (1822—1888) took a much narrower field for his investigations than Buckle; he confined himself to the subject of laws and institutions. His process of work was very much the same as that pursued by Charles Darwin in his *Origin of Species*. A law or an institution was for him a point in a process of evolution, and, however ancient it might be, he regarded it as something which had a vital bearing upon the present. He no more recognised a break in the generations of laws and institutions, than Darwin did in the lives of animals and men.

Walter Bagehot (1826—1877), the youngest of the group, differed from both. He was the exceptional man who found business "much more amusing than pleasure," and he is probably the only writer who ever made the Stock Exchange entertaining to the public who are not interested in shares and stocks. Clough, the poet, was at University College, London, when Bagehot was a student there, and he gave the young financier the literary interests which might otherwise have been left out of his education. Perhaps he helped to impart also that power of terse and pointed expression which enables Bagehot to put familiar truths in a memorable way, as when he tells us that "a constitutional statesman is in general a man of common opinions and uncommon abilities." He certainly did not impart that wit and humour which from time to time lights up his pupil's wisdom, as in the irresistible description of the schoolmaster: "A schoolmaster should have an atmosphere of awe, and walk wonderingly, as if he was amazed at being himself."

The subjects on which Bagehot had been training himself for years to write are treated in his book called *Lombard Street, a Description of the Money Market*, and in his *English Constitution*. There is no other book on the English constitution comparable to his in interest for the general reader; there is no other book on the money market which is entertaining as well as instructive. These, with *Physics and Politics*, are his most important contributions to thought and literature.

§ 4. *Science*

We have now reached the fourth and last division of this chapter treating of the thinkers and writers upon abstruse subjects. At first sight it seems wayward to drag the work of men of science into a book upon English literature; but Ruskin, the foremost English critic of art, reproached the poet Wordsworth because "he could not understand that to break a rock with a hammer in search of crystal may sometimes be an act not disgraceful to human nature, and that to dissect a flower may sometimes be as proper as to dream over it." Ruskin's own criticism rests upon science; and this recognition by men of letters of the importance of scientific research, even as a means of culture for poets, is the outcome of the investigations of the nineteenth century. These investigations had the most profound effect upon the whole mind of man. From scientific experiments men slowly came to believe that all nature was under the reign of law, and that even the winds were the effect of causes which might be counted upon to act with regularity. It was only in the nineteenth century that geology ceased to be "catastrophic" and became "uniformitarian" or, in other words, that earthquakes and volcanoes ceased to be regarded as the main agents of change, and the conception of forces operating slowly, silently, invisibly, took their place. A change of view so far-reaching could not be without effect on literature.

For the present purpose it is sufficient to say that the man chiefly instrumental in bringing about this change of view was Sir Charles Lyell (1797—1875). In his *Principles of Geology* Lyell points out the changes wrought upon the surface of the earth by glacial action, rain and the deposit of mud by rivers. Charles Darwin (1809—1882), when he started on his voyage round the world in the ship *Beagle*, was advised by Henslow the botanist to take Lyell's book with him, but to be cautious about accepting his teaching. The warning was in vain, for at the first opportunity of geologising Darwin became convinced of the "immense superiority" of Lyell's views. But when Darwin applied similar conceptions to living beings Lyell would not at first willingly follow, because he could not bring himself to admit the, to him, degrading theory that man is descended from brutes; and this he saw must be the outcome of the theory of evolution. Yet Darwin's great idea of the modification of species by variations acted upon by external circumstances is in effect just an extension of Lyell's own; and so to Lyell, in great measure, is due the modern conception of the government of the world by regular laws.

Lyell has a place in literature because he was a great man of science; Hugh Miller (1802—1856), the stonemason, has a place in science because he was a great man of letters. He was too ill-trained to make great additions to theory; but his personality and his power of writing fine strong English make his name memorable. Miller's truthfulness is his chief asset in the sphere of science. He looked with his own eyes, and he faithfully described what he saw, so that even when his inferences were wrong his work was of value. His *Footprints of the Creator* is an answer to *Vestiges of the Natural History of the Creation*, published anonymously in 1844, and acknowledged forty years later to be the work of Robert Chambers, the junior member of the great Edinburgh publishing house of W. and R. Chambers. Both members of this house were active with their pens, but Robert is the more distinguished writer. When in 1823 he published his *Traditions of Edinburgh*, Scott asked with wonder where the boy had got his information. His *Vestiges* passed into ten editions in nine years. Its author had grasped the great idea of evolution, and he had the gift of writing in a popular way. Darwin thought the writing and arrangement of the book admirable, but its geology bad and its zoology far worse. It remained for him in his *Origin of Species* to arrange and formulate the idea which Chambers had broached, and to establish for us the most far-reaching theory of the century.

The idea of evolution, as has been pointed out, was not unknown before Darwin. More than one scientific researcher had touched it, and it had been introduced into philosophy by the Hegelians and by Herbert Spencer (1820—1903). The latter framed the Synthetic Philosophy to show how the universe was gradually developed from beginning to end, if it can be said to have an end. The books belonging to his system are entitled *First Principles*, *Principles of Biology*, *Principles of Sociology*, and *Principles of Ethics*. In them he seeks to explain the "continuous re-distribution of matter and motion." He maintains that there is no impassable division between the world of dead matter and the world of living things; and, similarly, that the vegetable world shades into the animal. Even people who are not scientific can at least see that there are plants, like the sensitive plant, which show powers similar to animal powers, and they know that some things which have animal life are, to their eyes, more like vegetables than animals. Spencer tries to show us grounds for believing that complex forms of life come out of simple ones. But his theory breaks off abruptly at the point which divides that which has life from that which has none, and the only thing which we are sure of is that he has not been able to tell us whence we came, or whither we are going. He and the French philosopher Comte took all knowledge for their province, and the very greatness of their conception of their task marks them as very extraordinary men. Darwin says of Spencer, "If he had trained himself to observe more, even if at the expense, by the law of balancement, of some thinking power, he would have been a wonderful man."

Darwin, less ambitious than Spencer, contented himself with attempting to demonstrate the theory of evolution within the sphere of life, animal and vegetable. He was the greatest biologist of the nineteenth century, and few literary men have written with more charm of expression. Darwin spent seven years at the Grammar School of Shrewsbury, where his interest in science manifested itself in chemical experiments, and brought upon him the nickname of "Gas." His father intended him for the medical profession, and sent him to prepare for it in the University of Edinburgh. He only remained there two years, for he could not endure the sight of blood, and the thought of taking part in an operation turned him from the work of a doctor. His next university was Cambridge, where he went to prepare for the Church. We are tempted to smile now at the idea; but it was said of him in after years that he possessed "the bump of reverence developed enough for ten priests." Darwin left Cambridge with no higher attainment than a pass degree; but he had acquired a friend in Henslow the botanist, had made a collection of beetles, and had formed at least a taste for the study of nature. Although the young scientist had learned little or nothing from the college lectures, which he describes as "fearfully and incredibly dull," he had been training himself for the work of his life. He found his chance when Fitzroy took him as naturalist on the *Beagle*, which was just starting for a voyage round the world. He owed this post to the friendship of Henslow, but he very nearly lost it because of the shape of his nose; he says that Fitzroy "doubted whether any one with my nose could possess sufficient energy and determination for the voyage." Darwin justified his nose, for he amassed on that voyage the material which was to form the basis of all his later work, and to enable him to furnish proof of the soundness of his theory of evolution. The influence of this voyage on him was incalculable; on his return his father, a trained observer, remarked that the very shape of his head was altered. Unfortunately, while giving him such rich material, it at the same time seriously undermined his constitution.

Darwin's mental growth was now nearly complete, and for the future the events of his life are chiefly the dates of the publication of his books. He married in 1839, and some time later moved from London to Down, in Kent, where he spent the rest of his life. He never allowed the ill-health, which was the consequence of the voyage in the *Beagle*, to daunt him in his search after scientific truth. In the twenty years of thought which Darwin gave to the question of the forms of life before he published his greatest book, *The Origin of Species*, he became more and more convinced that no form is absolutely stable and unchangeable. Animals and plants alike tend to vary from the type of their parents; and geology convinced him that in the long course of ages the variations became very great. For a while he could think of no explanation; but at last the reading of the book by Malthus upon the problem of population gave him the key. The central doctrine of that book is that population tends to increase faster than the food required to supply their needs. Darwin at once saw that such a tendency must result in a struggle for existence, in which those individuals which were best adapted to their circumstances would win. Hence the "survival of the fittest." The phrase belongs to Spencer, but the conception exactly fits Darwin's theory. Variation then gives certain living beings an advantage over others, and heredity tends to accumulate the variations until new species are formed. Darwin's own phrase for the process thus described was "natural selection." This he considered not the only, but by far the most important, force in the production of new species of plants and animals. The theory in its main outlines was clear in Darwin's mind nearly four years before he began to write upon it. When he did begin it was on a scale three or four times as great as that adopted in *The Origin of Species*; and yet even this was only an abstract of the materials he had collected. In 1858, when he was still engaged upon this work, Darwin received the famous essay of Mr A. R. Wallace, entitled *On the Tendency of Varieties to depart indefinitely from the Original Type.* It showed that Mr Wallace had simultaneously come to the same conclusion as Darwin. The rest of the story of this wonderful dual discovery is well known. An abstract from the MS of Darwin was published at the same time with the essay of Wallace; and the former began at once to re-write his book on a smaller scale. *The Origin of Species* was published in 1859. Its author was fifty, and he had devoted twenty years of his life to this great work—a devotion possible only because he had a private fortune. After this came *The Descent of Man*, and then a series of works illustrative mainly of various aspects of the theory of evolution. Darwin's latest publication was *The Formation of Vegetable Mould through the Action of Worms.* The enthusiasm with which this book was received seemed to its author almost "laughable," but it was no more than its due. The book is a simple direct narrative showing so clearly as to fascinate the reader the incalculable importance of the action of a creature so insignificant as the earthworm.

Darwin had no natural gifts of literary expression, but he felt the importance of being able to say exactly what he meant in the simplest words. He tried hard to cultivate this capacity: "No nigger," he says, "with lash over him could have worked harder at clearness than I have done." He had his reward, for few authors have attained a higher mastery of the power of simple attractive narration. With no pretence to the brilliancy of Huxley, he had a wonderful power of making plain even to the uninstructed the technicalities of science. Doubtless his strict adherence to truth helped towards this result.

Thomas Henry Huxley (1825—1895) says that he took upon himself the post of "Darwin's bulldog, or maid-of-all-work and gladiator-general of science." By this assumption of service Huxley brought himself into prominence as a fighter for truth and became one of the chief agents in the diffusion of evolutionary ideas. He felt the joy of battle. But through all his many controversies he was steadily working in laboratories and talking in lecture rooms. He was in many ways the complement of Darwin. The latter knew little anatomy, while Huxley was a trained and accomplished anatomist; and this knowledge enabled him to supplement the evidence Darwin had adduced, and to combat criticism of him with success. For example, Huxley was able both to give and to justify a direct contradiction to the assertion of Richard Owen at the famous meeting of the British Association in 1860, that the difference between the brain of a man and that of the highest ape was greater than the difference between the brains of the highest and lowest quadrumana. But if Huxley did much for Darwin, he in turn gained from *The Origin of Species* a new reason, it might almost be said, for living; for in the service of the theory he found employment for his great stores of knowledge. His place in literature depends principally upon the essays and lectures in which he brings science to bear upon the interpretation of life and criticises old beliefs.

§ 1. *Carlyle.*

Thomas Carlyle, 1795—1881.
Life of Schiller, 1823—1824.
Wilhelm Meister's Apprenticeship (translation), 1824.
Sartor Resartus, 1833—1834.
The French Revolution, 1837.
Chartism, 1839.
Heroes and Hero-Worship, 1840.
Past and Present, 1843.
Oliver Cromwell's Letters and Speeches, 1845.
Latter-Day Pamphlets, 1850.
Life of Sterling, 1857.
Frederick the Great, 1858—1865.

§ 2. *The Theologians.*

Thomas Chalmers, 1780—1847.
Discourses on the Christian Revelation, 1817.
Edward Irving, 1792—1834.
John Henry Newman, 1801—1890.
The Arians of the Fourth Century, 1833.
Tracts for the Times (with others), 1833—1849.
Lyra Apostolica (with others), 1836.
An Essay on the Miracles recorded in the Ecclesiastical History of the Early Ages, 1843.
The Development of Christian Doctrine, 1845.
Loss and Gain, 1848.
Callista, 1856.
Apologia pro Vita Sua, 1864.
The Dream of Gerontius, 1865.
Verses on Various Occasions, 1868.
A Grammar of Assent, 1870.
John Keble, 1792—1866.
Life of Bishop Wilson, 1863.
Edward Bouverie Pusey, 1806—1882.
Historical Enquiry into the causes of the Rationalist Character of German Theology, 1828—1830.

Richard Whately, 1787—1863.
Logic, 1826.
Rhetoric, 1828.
Essays on some Difficulties in Paul, 1828.
Essays on the Errors of Romanism, 1830.
The Kingdom of Christ Delineated, 1841.
Thomas Arnold, 1795—1842.
The Principles of Church Reform, 1833.
History of Rome, 1838—1843.
Connop Thirlwall, 1797—1875.
History of Greece, 1835—1847.
Benjamin Jowett, 1817—1893.
Epistles to the Thessalonians, Galatians, and Romans, 1855.
The Dialogues of Plato, 1871.
Arthur Penrhyn Stanley, 1815—1881.
Life of Thomas Arnold, 1844.
Epistles to the Corinthians, 1855.
Sinai and Palestine, 1856.
Lectures on the History of the Eastern Church, 1861.
Lectures on the History of the Jewish Church, 1863—1865.
Richard William Church, 1815—1889.
St Anselm, 1870.
Dante, 1879.
Spenser, 1879.
Bacon, 1884.
The Oxford Movement, 1891.

§ 3. *The Philosophers.*

William Hamilton, 1788—1856.
Discussions on Philosophy and Literature, 1852.
Lectures on Metaphysics and Logic, 1859—1861.
Henry Longueville Mansel, 1820—1871.
Prolegomena Logica, 1851.
The Limits of Religious Thought, 1859.
The Philosophy of the Conditioned, 1866.
John Stuart Mill, 1806—1873.
A System of Logic, 1843.
The Principles of Political Economy, 1848.
On Liberty, 1859.
Representative Government, 1861.

Utilitarianism, 1863.
Comte and Positivism, 1865.
An Examination of Sir W. Hamilton's Philosophy, 1865.
The Subjection of Women, 1869.
Autobiography, 1873.

Henry Sidgwick, 1838—1900.
The Methods of Ethics, 1874.
The Principles of Political Economy, 1883.
The Elements of Politics, 1891.

Harriet Martineau, 1802—1876.
Illustrations of Political Economy, 1832—1834.
Deerbrook, 1839.
The Positive Philosophy of Auguste Comte freely translated and condensed, 1853.
History of England during the Thirty Years' Peace, 1849—1850.

George Henry Lewes, 1817—1878.
A Biographical History of Philosophy, 1845—1846.
Comte's Philosophy of the Sciences, 1853.
Life of Goethe, 1855.
Problems of Life and Mind, 1874—1879.

Thomas Hill Green, 1836—1882.
The Works of Hume (edited), 1874—1875.
Prolegomena to Ethics, 1883.

Edward Caird, 1835—1908.
A Critical Account of the Philosophy of Kant, 1877.
The Evolution of Religion, 1893.
The Evolution of Theology in the Greek Philosophers, 1904.

James Martineau, 1805—1900.
Rationale of Religious Inquiry, 1836.
Studies of Christianity, 1858.
Types of Ethical Theory, 1885.
The Seat of Authority in Religion, 1890.

Francis William Newman, 1805—1897.
Phases of Faith, 1850.

Henry Thomas Buckle, 1821—1862.
History of Civilization, 1857—1866.

Henry Sumner Maine, 1822—1888.
Ancient Law, 1861.
Village Communities, 1871.
The Early History of Institutions, 1875.
Popular Government, 1885.

Walter Bagehot, 1826—1877.
The English Constitution, 1865—1867.
Physics and Politics, 1872.
Lombard Street, 1873.

§ 4. *Science.*

Charles Lyell, 1797—1875.
Principles of Geology, 1830—1833.
Geological Evidences of the Antiquity of Man, 1863.
Hugh Miller, 1802—1856.
The Old Red Sandstone, 1840.
Footprints of the Creator, 1849.
My Schools and Schoolmasters, 1854.
The Testimony of the Rocks, 1857.
Robert Chambers, 1802—1871.
Vestiges of the Natural History of Creation, 1844.
Herbert Spencer, 1820—1903.
Principles of Psychology, 1855.
First Principles, 1862.
Principles of Biology, 1864—1867.
Principles of Sociology, 1876—1896.
Principles of Ethics, 1892—1893.
Charles Darwin, 1809—1882.
Journal of Researches during the Voyage of the Beagle, 1839.
The Structure and Distribution of Coral Reefs, 1842.
The Origin of Species, 1859.
The Descent of Man, 1871.
The Formation of Vegetable Mould through the Action of Worms, 1881.
Thomas Henry Huxley, 1825—1895.
Lay Sermons, 1870.
Hume, 1879.

CHAPTER II

POETRY

§ 1. *Some Pre-Victorian Poets*

PHILOSOPHERS and men of science stand upon the outskirts of literature; the poets occupy its very citadel, and the principal function of a book of criticism is to discuss poetry. The Victorian era was made illustrious by some very great ones, but its opening was comparatively unpromising, and we have first to discuss some who must be described as minor poets. They filled up the interval between the poets of the revolutionary period and the rise of the great luminaries of the Victorian era.

Before the end of the first quarter of last century two unlettered poets, Ebenezer Elliott (1781—1849) and John Clare (1793—1864), had begun to write. Both found in Thomson's *Seasons* the model for their early work, and both drew from nature their first inspiration. The picture of a primrose in a book of botany awoke Elliott to the beauties of nature, and the rhymes of a poor old woman with a memory stocked with verse helped to develop the poetic taste of Clare.

Ebenezer Elliott wrote his first poem, *A Vernal Walk*, at the age of seventeen. The impulse called the return to nature, a phase of the romance movement, which at this time inspired Wordsworth and Coleridge to write their

Lyrical Ballads, had touched the young iron-worker Elliott as well. But he had, as he claims, "a hand to do and a head to plan," and, without losing his love of nature, he was deeply interested in the industrial problems of his time and in the struggle of the democracy for political and social recognition. England was impoverished and exhausted by the long wars with Napoleon. Bread was exceedingly dear, and the poor had little money to pay for it. To Elliott the tax upon this necessary seemed the extreme of the tyranny of wealth, and, keenly sensitive to the misery around him, he devoted himself to the task of reform. In his eyes the landowners alone were the oppressors: against them as the common foe he saw himself, the iron-master, ranged side by side with his workmen. To every other evil of the industrial system he was blind. There is no hint in his verse of that conflict between master and man which is so familiar in the present day. And yet the struggle against the introduction of machinery had shown before Elliott's day how bitter, under the wages system, may be the strife between capital and labour. It was in this state of mind—wide awake to one phase of the problem and utterly blind to the other—that Elliott became the lyrist of the cause of labour. Fierce anger against the wrongdoer and deep pity for the wronged inspired his masterpiece, "Day, like our souls, is fiercely dark." Elliott's *Corn-law Rhymes* attracted the attention of Carlyle, who likens the poet's work to "lines of joy and harmony wrought out of troublous tears."

John Clare, the contemporary of Elliott, had a life full of sadness. At seven he had to earn his daily bread, and a little later out of his scanty earnings he paid the fees for his education at a night school. Soon he began to write, and all the odd scraps of paper which came his way were filled with verses. His mother found them and, indignant at this waste of time, used them to light her fire. At a lime kiln, where he found temporary employment, the master suspected that he neglected his work in order to write, and dismissed him. But the poetry which his own people despised drew at last the attention of men who understood its value, and in 1820 *Poems, descriptive of Rural Life* appeared. Southey, one of the Lake Poets, as they were called, spoke well of the work in *The Quarterly Review*. The peasant poet was taken to London, and fortune seemed about to smile upon him. A subscription was raised and £45 a year secured to him for life. He made his home in his native county of Northampton. But Clare was destined neither to be happy nor to remain fit to do his work. He drank too much, and his mind gave way, though probably not because of the drink. The last twenty-two years of his life were spent in an asylum; but, strange to tell, these were the years in which he did his finest work. Then, in particular, he wrote a lyric which his biographer, Martin, rightly calls "a sublime burst of poetry":

"I am, yet what I am none cares or knows."

This lyric by the poor lunatic is not only poetically the finest, but intellectually the strongest of all Clare's writings. "There are more things in heaven and earth than are dreamed of in our philosophy."

There is much in the literature of the earlier part of the Victorian era that bears witness how wide and how deep was the sense of the suffering and of the evils on which Elliott looked. The evidence may be found in prose and in poetry; in the grave works of Carlyle and Maurice, in the novels of Dickens, of Charles Kingsley, and of Mrs Gaskell. Mrs Browning's heart-rending *Cry of the Children* is a wail of innocent weakness in the grasp of overwhelming strength. The same sentiment inspires two notable poems of Thomas Hood (1799—1845), the most gifted poet between Shelley and Keats on the one hand and Tennyson and

Browning on the other. Hood started life as an engineer, but after a short apprenticeship to the trade his delicate health compelled him to seek work which gave him more rest. He ended by becoming at twenty-two sub-editor to *The London Magazine*, the periodical in which the essays of Charles Lamb and De Quincey's *English Opium-Eater* appeared. Hood never enjoyed affluence, and when he was thirty-five he lost practically everything through the failure of a firm in which he was interested. Hoping to pay off his debts by living economically abroad, he crossed to Holland; but the passage was so rough that he never recovered from the effects of it. The rest of his life was a struggle with poverty and disease. Sir Robert Peel gave him a pension of £100, which he only lived to enjoy for one year. In spite of ill-health and poverty Hood managed to be gay. In his kitchen he enjoyed playing pranks upon his wife, exciting her anxieties by declaring that the red and yellow spots on the plaice she was cooking for dinner indicated decomposition and made it dangerous for the family to eat. It would however be a mistake to regard Hood as merely a jester. He was essentially serious, but he had to live, and he found it best to be "a lively Hood for a livelihood."

Hood had, as the great man usually has, the capacity to develop. There are beautiful pieces—for example, *Ruth*—to be found among his early poems. But for his greatest work we must look onwards to the end. Perhaps the most poetical of all his writings is *The Haunted House*, a piece hardly surpassed in respect of success in producing the effect which the author wishes to produce. This and the two great poems dedicated to social problems, *The Bridge of Sighs* and *The Song of the Shirt*, are Hood's surest title to fame. With a sound instinct he directed that the words "*He sang the Song of the Shirt*" should be engraved on his tombstone; and Thackeray, referring to the fact that *The*

Bridge of Sighs was published just before the poet's death, wrote that this was "his Corunna, his Heights of Abraham—sick, weak, wounded, he fell in the full blaze of that great victory."

Very different from Hood was his contemporary, the irresponsible Hartley Coleridge (1796—1849). He had more affinity to the madhouse poet Clare. Hartley was the son of Samuel Taylor Coleridge, and along with the genius of his father he inherited the weakness of his father's character. Hartley was cradled in beauty and poetry, but no effort was made to give him self-control or will-power. This want of discipline led to the excesses in drink which deprived him of his fellowship at Oriel College, Oxford, and left him to end his days "wandering like a breeze" among the Cumberland lakes. "Lil' Hartley o' the Nab" the villagers called him, and they believed him to be a much greater writer than Wordsworth, who lived close by him at Rydal Mount. Hartley never grew up. In his own language he was still a child even when he was old. His genius was great, but the weakness of his nature made any long and serious work impossible. In his sonnets we have however some exquisite poetry, and in his *Biographia Borealis* some delightful reading.

There flourished during the same years a number of writers of religious verse who must be noticed. Yet the notice must be brief, for, though the spirit of our highest poetry is essentially religious, in our religious verse we do not find the highest poetry. The Hebrews knew how to write poetic psalms and hymns, but this gift has been denied to modern nations. James Montgomery (1771—1854), Reginald Heber (1783—1826) and John Keble are names which stand out among those of the hymn writers of this period. Montgomery has given us the familiar *Hail to the Lord's Anointed* and *For ever with the Lord.* In his numerous volumes of verse there are some grains of gold, but no work of the highest order. He is chiefly interesting as the mouthpiece of the spirit of the free churches, and takes his place here in contrast with John Keble, who did for the English Church party what Montgomery did for the Nonconformists. Heber stands between these two, and has further interest for us because of his slight contact with Sir Walter Scott. Heber met Scott in Oxford in 1803, when he had just won the prize for his poem *Palestine.* He read it to Scott, and at Scott's suggestion the famous lines describing the silent rise of Solomon's temple were added—"No hammer fell, no ponderous axes rung." Though the literary promise which Scott detected in the young man was never realised Heber is one of the best of modern hymnologists. But the main stream of religious verse at this period ran in the channel of the Oxford Movement, and in some ways the most important contributor to it was John Keble. Though his *Lyra Innocentium* has greater poetry, his *Christian Year* is, as has already been said, the book by which Keble will be best remembered. It is written to fit the fasts and festivals of the prayer-book, and the author's muse is hampered by the restrictions of the plan. On the other hand, this plan has added to its attractions for the devout reader and accounts for no small part of its popularity. Wordsworth criticised the volume in characteristic manner: "It is very good," he said, "so good, that, if it were mine, I would write it all over again."

There remain in the period under consideration a number of writers who, while differing widely in many things, are bound together by a common interest in the drama. But they produced no great dramas, because the requisite qualities were not united in any one man. Beddoes had plenty of poetry and Sheridan Knowles had technical skill; but it would have required the union of the two to produce a great dramatist.

James Sheridan Knowles (1784—1862) was trained to the medical profession, but he deserted it in 1809 and became an actor. He had great facility in the construction of plots, and could sustain the interest until the dénouement. But he had no poetry, no conception of Wordsworth's "light that never was on sea or land." This lack of poetry was fatal to him in tragedy. By a happy chance however in the middle of his life he turned to comedy, and *The Beggar's Daughter of Bethnal Green*, *The Hunchback*, *The Love Chase* and *Old Maids* are good examples of his work.

Of Knowles's contemporaries who wrote plays, several are now remembered for work of a different sort. In the case of Henry Hart Milman, the fame of the historian overshadows that of the dramatist; and though Mary Russell Mitford valued herself mainly as a tragedian and was thought to stand in the first rank, we remember her now only as the author of the exquisite sketches in *Our Village*. The name of James Robinson Planché would hardly deserve mention for the sake of his comedies and burlesques; but the reformer of the costume of the stage should not be wholly forgotten. It was he who substituted for the former haphazard style of dress a studied attempt to represent upon the stage the garb of the time in which the action of the play is laid. It was on the revival of *King John* in 1823 that the effect of his reform was first seen.

But comparatively barren of drama as the period is, there are a few writers who are dramatists or nothing, and a few others whose dramatic work cannot be ignored. Sir Aubrey de Vere (1788—1846) is memorable for his fine tragedy, *Mary Tudor*, which was ranked by Gladstone next to Shakespeare, and is good enough to afford at least some justification even for that emphatic praise. For distinct and sometimes subtle characterisation and for excellence of plot, *Mary Tudor* is among the best of the small group of poetical dramas of the Victorian period. It was written in the last year of De Vere's life and was published posthumously. But the author was a contemporary of Byron at Harrow, and two earlier and less excellent dramas give him a place among the writers now under discussion. His association with Byron renders all the more remarkable De Vere's complete freedom from the dominant influence of his early manhood. He was rather a Wordsworthian than a follower of Byron.

In his aloofness from Byron De Vere resembles Henry, afterwards Sir Henry, Taylor (1800—1886), who may be regarded as the leading representative at this period of what may be called the intellectual drama. Taylor's best, as well as his best-known, work is *Philip van Artevelde*, a play which is interesting not only for its intrinsic merit, but as a studied and deliberate embodiment of a theory. Taylor held that poetry had been tempted by Byron into the indulgence of sensation at the expense of intellect, and that the evil had been intensified in proportion as Byron's followers were weaker than and inferior to Byron himself. Taylor therefore proposed to himself to re-embody in poetry what he called its intellectual and immortal part, its philosophy. The design was admirable, but Taylor was not quite great enough to execute it with success. He himself underrated, if he did not forget, another element in poetry—that which is called "inspiration." His characters are constructed rather than created.

If however success be the test of merit, *the* dramatist of the period is not any of those who have been named, but Bulwer Lytton. He will fall to be considered more fully as a novelist, but the author of two of the very small number of plays which have kept the stage from that day to this cannot be ignored as a dramatist. His *Lady of Lyons* was written in two weeks for the actor Macready, and became a dazzling success. The plot is absurd, and the hero, Claude Melnotte, incredibly silly. *Richelieu* was, and still is, almost equally popular. The author of these plays has a fascinating though grandiloquent manner, which harmonises with the glare of the footlights. His taste is false, his sentiment is false, and his characters are artificial; yet, notwithstanding all this, his plays have that something which makes them go. It is more surprising that he shows a true lyrical gift, and that what in him is meretricious is less offensive in his lyrics than it is in his dramas.

In strong contrast to Taylor as well as to Lytton stands the group of men who may be called poets of the Elizabethan revival. The greatest of these was Thomas Lovell Beddoes (1803—1849). He has been called a Gothic Keats, but there is in his poetry a note of Shelley as well as a strain of Keats. More remarkable than either is his similarity in tone to the Elizabethans. This was probably due to natural kinship rather than to conscious imitation; for Beddoes had no faith in imitation or in revivals of any sort. While he was an undergraduate at Oxford his first literary ventures, *The Improvisatore* and *The Bride's Tragedy*, appeared. He meant to make literature his profession, and four years later he announced to his friend Kelsall the completion of "a very Gothic-styled tragedy" called *Death's Jest-Book*. But after the two former early works only one or two short poems were published during his lifetime. He recognised that he would never be a popular dramatist, and suddenly resolved to abandon literature in favour of medicine, the profession of his father. This resolution led to his residence abroad, and he spent the rest of his life either in Germany or in Switzerland. He ultimately died by his own hand in the hospital at Basle. His blank verse can be noble and his lyrics beautiful, but his plays can never be acted because they are utterly chaotic.

§ 2. *Tennyson*

Tennyson has put on record his feeling of irreparable loss on the death of Byron, and the Carlyles were affected almost as deeply. Some ten years later Wordsworth in a well-known poem lamented the death of one after another of the giants of the past generation. Such utterances show us what was the view taken by men on the verge of the Victorian period as to the state of literature in their day. To them it seemed a time destitute of genius. The writers who have just been discussed were not the equals of the giants of the past, and no contemporary could be sure that among living men there was any equal to them. But when we look back we can see that, among the poets, two of the younger men were quite worthy to be set beside the great men of the revolutionary period. The two in question were, of course, Tennyson and Browning.

Alfred Tennyson (1809—1892) was the third son of the rector of Somersby in Lincolnshire, and his father was the son of the vicar of the neighbouring parish of Louth. In his childhood Tennyson was shy, retiring, imaginative, but neither an entertaining nor an attractive boy. Lady Ritchie, the daughter of Thackeray, tells a story of him at five years old playing in the vicarage garden. The wind caught his pinafore and whirled him along, and helpless, breathless, he shouted out, "I hear a voice that's speaking in the wind." Those nine words must have been his first line of poetry. His next verses took the form of an elegy written upon the death of his grandmother. His grandfather paid him ten shillings for the poem, adding, "that is the first money, my boy, that you have made by poetry,—and take my word, it will be the last." The next earnings came through a Louth publisher, who offered ten pounds for a collection of one hundred and two poems published under the name of *Poems by Two Brothers*. The authors were really three in number, as both his two elder brothers, Frederick and Charles Tennyson, joined with Alfred in this early venture. They spent the money in making a tour through Lincolnshire to examine the beautiful architecture of its old churches.

The Tennysons' home was in the midst of the most peaceful English scenery, where the family of eight sons and four daughters, with their parents, made a society in itself. Tennyson may have had Somersby rectory in his mind when he speaks of the "English home" in *The Palace of Art* as "a haunt of ancient Peace." The seclusion of the place was so profound that even the news of the battle of Waterloo took long to reach it. This retirement, and the fact that the Tennysons were educated at home, helps to explain the almost gruff reserve which through life marked the shy manners of the poet. Their father prepared his sons for Trinity College, Cambridge. He must have been remarkable in his way, but the impression he produced on the mind of his old housekeeper was merely that of a man "glowering" in his study, the walls of which were covered "wi' 'eathen gods and goddesses wi'out cloäs." Alfred in those days was best known as the champion athlete who came down to the village green and beat the rustic competitors in their own games.

His removal from these early surroundings took place in 1828, when he matriculated at Trinity College, Cambridge. He found his two elder brothers already established there. At first he was too shy to participate in College society; but a few months served to break the barriers down, his genius was discovered, and he became part of a group of youthful enthusiasts who have come down in history as "The Apostles" of Cambridge. They chose this name because there were twelve of them. Among them were Richard Monckton Milnes, afterwards Lord Houghton,

Trench, who became an archbishop, F. D. Maurice, and Arthur Henry Hallam, whom Tennyson in *In Memoriam* describes as "the master bowman of the group." This acquaintance with Hallam ripened into a friendship as warm as the love between David and Jonathan. Tennyson says, "Arthur Hallam was as near perfection as mortal could be, and his was such a lovely nature that he had nothing to learn from life." He became betrothed to Emily, the sister of his friend, and his early death at twenty-two was almost as heavy a blow to her brother as to her. Hallam left little writing to indicate the greatness of his powers, he had not time in his short life, but his influence over Tennyson was far-reaching. After his death the whole tone of Tennyson's poetry changed. He has the same exquisite touch, but the playful frivolities disappear, and he seems full of serious purpose in all he writes.

Two years before the death of Hallam the discipline of sorrow had begun for Tennyson. The old home at Somersby was broken up by the death of his father in 1831. Alfred had left college without taking a degree, and his prospects of earning a living at this time were so poor that his engagement with Emily Sellwood had to be broken off. After this separation the lovers did not meet for ten years, when the success of *In Memoriam* made it possible for the poet to offer her a home. Tennyson's marriage was soon followed by his appointment to the office of laureate. He was formally installed as the successor of Wordsworth in 1850. He dressed for the ceremony at the house of Samuel Rogers and borrowed the velvet court dress and sword of his host. It is curious that his predecessor, Wordsworth, had dressed at the same house and had borrowed the same garb. After these two events the history of Tennyson's life is marked only by the publication of his works. There are occasional visits to London; but in his later years his time was chiefly spent in his two country houses, one at Freshwater in the Isle of Wight, and the other in the beautiful Surrey scenery of Haslemere.

In 1842 Tennyson published *Poems* in two volumes. One volume was filled almost entirely with pieces which had appeared in the *Poems* of 1830 and 1832, but the second contained only two poems which were not new. This second volume marked a great development. Many of the best of his shorter poems are here, and it is in his shorter poems that Tennyson excels. No one ever studied more carefully the art of writing them. "Every short poem," he says, "should have a definite shape, like the curve, sometimes a single, sometimes a double one, assumed by a severed tress, or the rind of an apple when flung upon the floor." In this collection, at which he had worked for nine years, we find the Arthurian poems of *Sir Galahad*, *Sir Launcelot*, *Queen Guinevere* and *Morte d'Arthur*. It contains also the classical idyll of *Ulysses*, *The Two Voices*, *The Vision of Sin*, *The Palace of Art*, *Locksley Hall*, *The Lotos Eaters*, *St Agnes' Eve* and the exquisite song *Break, break, break*. There are, in fact, specimens of nearly every kind of verse except the dramatic, and of these not a few are among the finest things in the whole range of Tennyson's work. His friend Edward FitzGerald thought that he never afterwards rose so high.

The Princess followed the *Poems* of 1842. It has won its way into English hearts by its six beautiful songs, but, as a whole, it is somewhat of a failure. It hovers midway between jest and earnest. From the many changes which were afterwards made in it, we may conclude that Tennyson himself was not satisfied. Its subject is the emancipation of women. But there was no place in Tennyson's world for the advanced modern woman. The sweet girl-graduates, whom he describes as pursuing learning in the retired atmosphere of a convent-like college, are no new creations of his pen. They are merely the Madelines, Rosalinds, and Marianas of his youthful poems, led, in Tennyson's eyes, astray by the new learning. The poet feels that their venture into the halls of science is all a mistake, and that marriage ought to be their final goal.

During the years after 1833 Tennyson read deeply and widely, and his poems bear witness to his careful study of the literatures of Greece and Rome, as well as those of the modern languages. His familiarity with science is attested by Norman Lockyer, who declared Tennyson's mind to be "saturated with astronomy"; while Huxley called him "the first poet since Lucretius who has understood the drift of science." He conceived it to be his mission to give in his *In Memoriam* a poetic version of the problems in thought and in religion which the recent discoveries of science had thrust upon the minds of men and women. Devout souls have found guidance in Tennyson's philosophy of life in this poem, and its words of hope and sympathy have restored peace and comfort to minds that felt that their faith had been cut away by science. It became extremely popular. It appealed to every one. The man of science was gratified to find that his point of view was understood, while the anxious Christian, filled with fears and doubts, recognised many of his own difficulties powerfully and beautifully expressed, and was cheered by the voice of hope in the last lines and the expression of faith that "*somehow* good will be the final goal of ill." The stanza of *In Memoriam* was used by Ben Jonson, but Tennyson practically discovered it over again and made it one of the best-known of English stanzas. Few poems have been more quoted than *In Memoriam.* It is full of "jewels five words long," and the literary allusions, reminiscences and turns of phrase give it a rare power of attraction.

The choice of Tennyson for the laureateship was a happy one. He has rarely been excelled in the art of writing verses to celebrate national events. The death of the great Duke of Wellington gave him the first opportunity, and the *Ode* which he wrote on this occasion is one of the noblest utterances of patriotism in verse. The Crimean war drew from him the stirring *Charge of the Light Brigade*, to be followed thirty years later by a far more skilful piece on a cognate theme, *The Charge of the Heavy Brigade*. The later and more beautiful poem has never been able to move the first from its place as popular favourite. So too the earlier *Locksley Hall* still holds the field, though *Locksley Hall Sixty Years After* is a weightier and more thoughtful poem. The one expresses the feelings of a youthful dreamer, the other the ripe experience of a great mind.

Through all these years Tennyson had been trying to write upon the old legends of King Arthur and his Round Table. The subject was not new. Milton had thought of it for the great work which was to justify his devoting his life to poetry, Spenser at an earlier date had made use of the legends, and Lytton had written an epic poem on Arthur. Indeed the Arthurian romances had captivated the imaginative minds of England, France and Germany, from the middle ages downwards. But it was reserved for Tennyson to gather the twelve new-old tales into one collection and to send them into the world as *The Idylls of the King*.

At an early date Tennyson wrote out prose sketches of the legends, but the first story to appear in verse was *Morte d'Arthur*. FitzGerald heard this poem read in 1835. It showed already a skill in the difficult measure of blank verse which Tennyson never afterwards surpassed. Except this no *Idylls* appeared for more than twenty years. But the poet had not laid the subject aside. In 1859 *Enid*, *Vivien*, *Elaine* and *Guinevere* were published. Then there was another pause of ten years before the appearance of

The Holy Grail and other Poems. Among the other poems were *The Coming of Arthur, Pelleas and Ettarre* and *The Passing of Arthur,* as *Morte d'Arthur* is now called. In 1871 appeared *The Last Tournament,* in 1872 *Gareth and Lynette,* and then, after a long interval, the centre of the group is reached in *Balin and Balan,* which came in 1885. There is thus no real unity in *The Idylls of the King.* Tennyson begins at the end of the tale, arrives at the beginning midway, and closes with the central episode. The twelve legends circle round the godlike Arthur, "the blameless King," a piece of colourless perfection who is rather a nineteenth century hero than a mediæval knight. He is modern, although his history is ancient. Tennyson had little sympathy with, or understanding of, the far-away ages. He derived the knowledge required for these poems from the translation of the *Mabinogion* by Lady Charlotte Guest, and from Malory's *Morte d'Arthur.* He borrowed much from these sources. For this he has been censured, but the blame is not just. These great stories of romance, handed down from early times, are the poetical inheritance of the world, they have a different message for each generation, and it is the privilege of new poets to express the message in the language of their times. The newcomer who prefers to invent rather than use the material that has come down to him may find that he has done himself a great wrong. Shakespeare acted on the same principle as Tennyson, and so did the great Greek tragedians.

The greatest flaw in *The Idylls of the King* is the unreality which clings to all the characters. Launcelot is interesting because of his human frailties, but, as a knight, even he is "faultily faultless." Vivien, the most degraded character, is a dull evil-doer when we compare her fascinations with the unprincipled witchery of Cleopatra, or the cleverness of Becky Sharp. The story most typical of the age of Arthur is *The Quest of the Grail.* It is an allegory, but Tennyson interprets it in a manner which is highly significant and altogether his own. To the mediæval inventor of the story, holiness was an absolute good, and evil could not come out of it. Tennyson makes the quest of the Grail a means towards the break-up of the Round Table. He felt that the quest after heaven which it describes, the withdrawal of man from life and its ordinary duties and his consecration to holiness, might be good for the Sir Galahads, but was a mere misleading Will-o'-the-wisp to the ordinary man, stained and spotted, yet capable of work useful to the world. He had no belief in pure saintliness for the average man. He felt that a man must be measured not by the absence of evil and wrong-doing, but by the presence of good. Seeing that he had this manly conception before his eyes, it is difficult to pardon the colourless perfection of King Arthur, or to put much faith in his efforts to right the wrong.

There is no trace of the dramatic gift in *The Idylls of the King*; that gift is singularly wanting in all Tennyson's early work; and he might never have discovered that he possessed it had he not conceived the idea of writing poems in dialect. *The Northern Farmer, Old Style* is founded upon the dying words of a farm bailiff, "God A'mighty little knows what He's about, a-taking me. An' Squire will be so mad an' all." Tennyson carried this expression in his mind for years, and also the text of the farmer of the new style, whose original was reported to have said, "When I canters my 'erse along the ramper (highway), I 'ears proputty, proputty, proputty." Then the delightful *Northern Cobbler* sprang from the story of a man who "set up a bottle of gin in his window when he gave up drinking, in order to defy the drink." Turning over the pages of the *Church-Warden and the Curate* we come upon lines full of delightful humour from Tennyson himself:

"If ever tha meäns to git 'igher,
Tha mun tackle the sins o' the wo'ld, an' not the faults o' the Squire."

The discovery of this new power of portraying character moved Tennyson towards the dramatic form, and this is one of the changes in the work of the last fifteen or twenty years of his life. He came to feel that the thoughts and experiences of his already long life could not be any longer cabined and confined in the twists of a severed tress, or the curl of an apple rind. His early poems had no theme which could be put into prose, but essays might be written on the subject of his later ones. The thought is weightier, and there is change in the diction and rhythm as well. The early poems are characterised by smoothness, the later ones by strength. Contrast the "moonshine maidens," as they have been called, of the *Poems* of 1830—Claribel, Lilian and the rest—with *Locksley Hall Sixty Years After.* That Tennyson could still write as smoothly as ever is shown by *Crossing the Bar* and the exquisite song, "To sleep, to sleep." But in these later days many of his themes did not permit such treatment. The heavier material he was handling demanded different words and different metre. The change was all a movement towards reality. Tennyson never became what is commonly understood by the phrase "a realist"; but he did in his old age come into much closer contact with the workaday world than in the beginning of his career. This line of development led Tennyson to the drama. This was the final step, and it was so unexpected that when his first play, *Queen Mary*, appeared in 1875 nearly all anticipated failure. And they were not mistaken. There was plenty of matter; but it was ill handled, the characters were not interesting, and the piece lacked poetry. *Harold* followed in 1876; and in 1884 *Becket, The Cup* and *The Falcon* showed that this poet approaching eighty had not lost his power to learn. The characters of Harold and Becket are well drawn, and in both plays

Tennyson was fortunate in his subject, but especially so in the case of the great prelate of Henry II's time. The struggle between Church and State in the fourteenth century, as represented by the personal conflict between King Henry and his bold subject, is one of the most dramatic in English history. Tennyson has skilfully contrasted these two chief actors in it, and yet revealed the likeness between them, showing Becket to be stronger than Henry by reason of the discipline which circumstances had given to the one and denied to the other. In the two women of this drama, Eleanor and Rosamond, his touch is no less sure. The gentle feminine dependence, loyalty and long-suffering of the latter give little cause for the cruel scorn of Eleanor, and leave us indignant with her harshness. The best part of ten years was given by Tennyson to these experiments in character-drawing. His early admirers grudged the time, but he judged better than they. He could hardly have surpassed himself in other forms of verse or added anything strikingly new; while in the plays which contain the characters of Harold, Becket, Eleanor, Rosamond, and Edith we have valuable additions to the dramatic portrait-gallery of England.

§ 3. *Browning*

Robert Browning (1812—1889), the most serious rival of Tennyson among the poets of the Victorian era, was reared in an atmosphere of learning, and, in the language of Oliver Wendell Holmes, grew up as familiar with books as a stable boy is with horses. The bookcases of his father's modest house in Clapham were filled with the best English, French, Greek and Latin authors. The elder Browning, who was a clerk in the Bank of England, found in them recreation and relief from the dull monotony of his daily work, and he had trained himself unknowingly to be abler than most fathers to cultivate and foster the genius of his gifted son. The Brownings were dissenters, and in the poet's childhood the Act of Uniformity still pressed its iron weight on the country and kept the best education for the sons of Churchmen. The public schools and the universities were closed to young Browning. But in his case this deprivation is hardly to be regretted; in fact it may have helped to strengthen the originality of mind for which he is distinguished. He would not have been a better poet had he won university distinctions, but he might have been a more conventional one. The elder Browning recognised the rare gifts of his boy and determined to make him an author by profession. This was the resolution of a big-minded man, for he knew from his own wide reading that the preparation for this task of making books is expensive and prolonged and the prizes to be won in it few, while even moderate success is uncertain and difficult to attain. His own income was small, but he was ready to venture it and his savings on his son. The boy took his profession very seriously, and we find him setting out to prepare himself by "reading and digesting the whole of Johnson's dictionary." Browning stands then with Milton among the very few Englishmen who have been deliberately dedicated to, and therefore educated for, the profession of literature. For three years he was taught by a private tutor, and for one session he attended lectures at the University of London, afterwards University College. His father then sent him to travel for a year, and he visited Russia and Italy, and drank in knowledge of all sorts. Even in art Rossetti compares his attainments with those of Ruskin to the disadvantage of the latter. "I found," he says, "his [Browning's] knowledge of early Italian art beyond that of anyone I ever met—*encyclopædically* beyond that of Ruskin himself."

When Browning was twelve years old his proud father

had gone to the expense of privately printing a volume of verses under the title of *Incondita.* Nine years later an aunt bore the cost of publishing *Pauline.* It is called "a fragment of a confession." The confession, which is the poet's own, reveals all his youthful ideals and his manner of training himself for his career. We also find there the idea that there is nothing of first importance in life except the growth of the soul. This conception governs the whole of his work to the end of his life; and to the end the development of the soul is the theme of his greatest works. Nothing else, he tells us, is worth study. Two years after *Pauline* Browning published *Paracelsus*, in some ways the most remarkable of all his works. He was only twenty-three, and yet he had reached almost his full literary stature. Had he advanced subsequently in a similar degree, he would have rivalled the first poet of all time. But in his development he differs from Tennyson. The latter grew in force and richness and in depth of meaning until the close of his long life, while Browning rarely wrote with greater power than in this, the first poem he was willing to acknowledge ; for in after-life he was ashamed of *Pauline* and only suffered it to be reprinted from fear of piracy.

In 1844 Browning married the poetess Elizabeth Barrett. She was an invalid and he practically carried her to the church in Euston Road, where they were married without the knowledge of her relatives. Their consent, the Brownings thought, it would be hopeless to ask; and subsequent events proved that they were right, for Mr Barrett thought that such a union was an outrage upon decency, and refused to grant his daughter his forgiveness. To put many miles between them and these unsympathetic relations the poet and his wife set up their home in Italy. There a son was born to them, and there they found inspiration for much of their most important work. After Mrs Browning's death in 1861 her husband came back to England; but his heart was in his adopted country, concerning which he had said, paraphrasing Queen Mary, that the word Italy would be found engraven in his heart. He went back to it in the end and died in the beautiful palace of his son upon the Grand Canal of Venice.

That we may fully understand Browning's work it is necessary to recognise the two great principles which run through it all. They are the principles of love and of knowledge; and he held that the greater is love. Paracelsus makes a failure of his life from his one-sided devotion to knowledge, which he looks upon as the gateway of power. He is like an Eastern carpet-weaver who should set to work believing that some one colour is the most beautiful of all, and that the whole web should consist of it. After nine weary years of isolation and toil he ends his experiments, convinced by his own failures that every colour has its own beauty, and that the business of life is to use them all and to find for each its place in the pattern.

These thoughts appear in all Browning's works; they are his philosophy of life. In *Paracelsus* he tries to keep his mind on the poet's side of the line that divides poetry from philosophy. But too often he strays beyond it. In this way his metaphysics often overloads his poetry and makes its meaning difficult. It certainly does so in *Sordello*. It is questionable whether this poem has ever been understood, and some have hinted that the author could explain it very little better than his critics. There is a well-known story that Douglas Jerrold, reading it in illness and finding himself utterly unable to take in its meaning, was thrown into a panic by the belief that he had lost his reason; and Harriet Martineau relates in her autobiography that for the same cause she thought she must be ill.

Paracelsus is a poem in dramatic form, but it is not a regular play. In 1837 however, at the suggestion of his friend Macready the actor, Browning wrote the drama of

Strafford, and for eight years the bulk of his work took the dramatic form. Six of the eight numbers of *Bells and Pomegranates* were plays—*King Victor and King Charles, The Return of the Druses, A Blot in the 'Scutcheon, Colombe's Birthday, Luria* and *A Soul's Tragedy*. Browning possessed in the highest degree some of the gifts of a dramatic genius, but he did not possess all. For this reason his plays have failed to keep the stage. Their chief defect is want of action. We are always either looking backward at some great tragedy which has taken place, or waiting outside helpless while another is being perpetrated. Much is said but little is done.

Browning at last realised that for him there were none of the solid rewards of a successful playwright, and diverted his mind to the production of those dramatic monologues which gave the best expression to his very original intellect. Each character gives its own version of the story in which he has played a part. This is the prevalent form in the remaining two numbers of *Bells and Pomegranates*, namely, *Dramatic Lyrics* and *Dramatic Romances and Lyrics*. The poems so entitled are of many kinds. Two, *The Pied Piper of Hamelin* and *How they brought the Good News from Ghent to Aix*, are most spirited narratives; some, like *Home Thoughts from Abroad* and *Home Thoughts from the Sea*, are expressions of the poet's own emotion; but most of them are intensely vivid studies of character, generally in some moment of crisis. Such are *In a Gondola, Porphyria's Lover, The Flight of the Duchess*, and *The Bishop orders his Tomb at St Praxed's Church*. Of the last-named poem Ruskin wrote, "I know no other piece of English prose or poetry, in which there is so much told, as in these lines, of the Renaissance spirit—its worldliness, pride, hypocrisy, ignorance of itself, love of art, of luxury, and of good Latin."

After *Bells and Pomegranates* came *Christmas Eve and*

Easter Day. These poems were written at a time when religious questions were disturbing England in general and Oxford in particular; and now humorously, now in serious fashion, they contributed the poet's criticism of the religious unrest. The scenes we see in *Christmas Eve* are a Nonconformist chapel, St Peter's in Rome and a German freethinker's lecture room. They are the centres of some delightful pictures, half pathetic, half laughable. In the dissenting congregation there is "the fat weary woman," with her umbrella a wreck of whalebones, and "the little old-faced, peaking, sister-turned-mother" of the sickly babe, who has trudged to chapel through the rain and is now adding "her tribute to the door-mat sopping." Then,

> "By the creaking rail to the lecture-desk,
> Step by step, deliberate
> Because of his cranium's over-freight,"

we see "the hawk-nosed, high-cheek-boned professor" mount to the desk, where he proceeds to exhaust faith, as air is pumped atom by atom from an air-bell.

This poem and the companion piece are, for Browning, singularly free from entanglement, and so is the collection called *Men and Women*, in which are included the exquisite verses, *One Word More*, addressed to his wife:

> "There they are, my fifty men and women
> Naming me the fifty poems finished!
> Take them, Love, the book and me together:
> Where the heart lies, let the brain lie also."

Christmas Eve and *Easter Day* form part of a group of poems which cover nearly the whole of religious thought. Others are to be found in the collection just mentioned, *Men and Women*, and others again in *Dramatis Personae*. In this group we have pictures of the soul of the primitive man groping for something to worship and fashioning his god in his own rude image. Such is Caliban, the speaker in *Caliban upon Setebos*. In *Cleon* we have taken an enormous stride onwards. The speaker is a polished Greek, sceptical, but lured by the thought of the immortal life promised by the barbarian Paul to whoever will become a Christian. But *Cleon* argues that were this idea true, Jove would surely have revealed it to the Greeks. Karshish is the learned Arabian doctor who, having seen and talked with the newly raised Lazarus, stands attracted by Christ's character, but repelled by the miracle worked in the tomb. In *Caliban upon Setebos* Browning will have us realise that the god of our conception is apt to be a god of our own creation. Setebos is the being worshipped by Caliban, and his nature is cruel as Caliban's own. In *Saul* the speaker is David, and the subject is the coming of the Messiah. But it is in *Rabbi Ben Ezra* that we hear Browning's clearest song of faith. The Rabbi is an old man, the type of all that is best and wisest in his race, and so his ideals are fit for either Jew or Gentile. Browning would have us see that the purest religion is of any creed or none. In the Pope in *The Ring and the Book* we have another Ben Ezra. They are both aged men, standing on the brink of eternity. They are represented as giving expression to their inner-most beliefs, and these are identical, although one speaker is a Jewish Rabbi, and the other the head of the Catholic Church. They welcome pain and doubt as signs of our near kinship with God, and they hail failure and disap-pointment as a stimulus to make us rise above ourselves. The Rabbi welcomes "each rebuff that turns earth's smooth-ness rough." Better high aim than low achievement, he says ; and Abt Vogler repeats the same teaching. High effort that has proved too high and resulted in failure, heroic struggle that has been too hard and has ended in defeat, these are "music sent up to God" ; it is "enough that He heard it once : we shall hear it by and by."

Browning's next publication after the *Dramatis Personae*, to which the poems last mentioned belong, was *The Ring and the Book.* It had occupied him for six years. There are four principal characters in the story—Count Guido, the husband and murderer of Pompilia the girl-wife, Pompilia herself, the priest Caponsacchi, who helps her to escape from Guido, and the Pope, who examines the evidence and pronounces judgment upon the criminal. The story is told in turn by each of these characters. There are other speakers as well, but only the books devoted to these four characters are really great. Browning shows us the husband, Count Guido, in two wholly different aspects. On the first occasion he is the great noble, the polished Italian gentleman. He touches, half with pride, half with apology, upon his vices—they are the faults of his age and station, he is no worse than others of his rank. When he is tortured in order to extract the truth, he bears his sufferings with trained self-control and speaks of them with dignified restraint. He argues his case with his judges as between one man of birth and another, touching gently but with wily cunning upon the services of himself and his house to the Church. Throughout this scene he is well-bred, courteous, restrained, deferential. After he is condemned and is convinced that all hope is over, we see before us the real Guido. His fine manners have fallen from him. The veneer of breeding is rubbed off. His whole life has been a lie, and nothing now remains but the brute.

Pompilia is the finest female character ever drawn by Browning. The aged Pope calls her "perfect in whiteness." He sees everywhere intellect, and energy, and knowledge—sees and admires; but "they make not up, I think, the marvel of a soul like thine." This sweet piece of womanhood is married to the evil-living Guido and shut up in his castle of Arezzo, where she lives a life of unmixed suffering. She is patient until there arises a question of right and wrong. "God plants us where we grow," she says and accepts quietly the miseries of her existence. But when she feels a new life awakening in her, the child that is to come, she turns to the Church for protection from her cruel husband. She must have outside help and guidance, and God's priest Caponsacchi must give it. Her childlike appeal for help is the salvation of Caponsacchi. He is not an evil-liver, but he loves pleasure, and the demand made upon him by Pompilia is the touchstone by which he is to be tested. Redeemed by her purity and innocence, his light easy-going nature is gradually crystallised into a rock of strength.

Of these five books *The Pope* is the finest. There is nothing grander in Browning than the picture of this aged man sitting in the seat of justice. He is himself on the brink of death, and feels the possibility that his judgment may be wrong. But there is no shrinking from his awful responsibility, no drawing back from his duty as God's vicar upon earth. In discharge of that duty he pronounces sentence :

> "Acquaint Count Guido and his fellows four
> They die to-morrow."

Then, as if in the end to justify the severe sentence, he adds,

> "I may die this very night
> And how should I dare die, this man let live?"

After *The Ring and the Book* was published in 1869 a change came over Browning, and, though he wrote much, little of his subsequent work rises to a high level as poetry. In the seventies his publications followed fast upon one another. At that time came *Prince Hohenstiel-Schwangau* and *Balaustion's Adventure*, *Fifine at the Fair*, *Red Cotton Night-Cap Country*, *The Inn Album* and two series of *Dramatic Idylls.* His Greek translations were another development of this period, the *Agamemnon* of Aeschylus and *Aristophanes' Apology.* On the whole the translations are not successful. Browning leaves these classics almost as difficult for the English reader as they are in the original Greek.

Browning's last work was *Asolando*. It came out almost at the moment of his death, and proclaimed again his faith that often through evil itself a higher good is won. Of himself he wrote as

"One who never turned his back but marched breast forward,
Never doubted clouds would break,
Never dreamed, though right was worsted, wrong would triumph,
Held we fall to rise, are baffled to fight better,
Sleep to wake."

§ 4. *Minor Singers*

The preceding sketch of the work of Tennyson and Browning shows that a considerable time had to pass before even they could make a deep impression upon their contemporaries. The taste for poetry had declined, and it was no easy task to revive it. Notwithstanding this, a great deal of poetry was written in the years between the advent of Tennyson and the middle of the century, and some of it was very good. But the whole mass is confusing, and the only means by which we may hope to find a path through it is by grouping the writers in classes. There were writers of ballads, of *vers de société*, of religious poetry, of philosophical poetry, of political poetry. There were besides two other groups, one of which must be noticed because of race, and the other because of sex—the Celtic poets and the women poets.

The ballad writers are the literary descendants of Sir Walter Scott, to whom the most important of them, Macaulay, in the preface to the *Lays of Ancient Rome*, acknowledges his indebtedness. Macaulay has been spoken of too harshly by Matthew Arnold, who calls his *Lays* "pinchbeck." The criticism is hardly just; Macaulay did not aim at writing sublime poetry, he tried to produce spirited verse and to make it live by his vivid narrative. And he succeeded. In these Roman ballads we hear the sound of trampling horses and of clashing arms, and surely we are richer for the emotions they produce. Another who followed the lead of Scott was William Edmonstoune Aytoun (1813—1865), the author of the *Lays of the Scottish Cavaliers.* Aytoun was a man of varied gifts. He wrote good criticisms, told excellent stories, and made most amusing parodies. The famous *Bon Gaultier Ballads* were the joint production of himself and of Theodore Martin. These belong to the sub-class of humorous ballads; and akin to them are the famous *Ingoldsby Legends* of R. H. Barham, of which *The Jackdaw of Rheims* is the best known. But the greater part of the witty verse of the period has lost its flavour. Hardly any task seems more difficult than to write amusing verse so that it shall retain its attractiveness for more than one generation; and when success is achieved it is because of humour rather than wit.

Few forms of literature are, in spirit, more sharply contrasted with the ballads than *vers de société.* In an unsophisticated age, when the art of delicate repartee and persiflage has not had time to be cultivated, the two could not be found together, because in such an age an artificial product like *vers de société* would be impossible. In the Victorian period the ballad was a revival. That epoch had behind it centuries of literary work. It would not be surprising therefore to find in it the highly-finished product we call *vers de société.* And in fact we do find Winthrop Mackworth Praed (1802—1839), who was probably the most skilful of all English writers in this form. Among earlier writers Praed's only serious rival is Prior. Praed began to write while he was still at school, and his early verses were printed in *The Etonian,* of which he was the chief supporter. He remained an active writer until the end of his life. But he seems to have recognised that there was a limit to his powers, for he never attempted anything deeply serious, and there is not much evidence that he would have succeeded had he made the attempt. We cannot say that he was prevented by his early death, for he lived as long as Burns, and much longer than Shelley and Keats. But the playful wit, ready sarcasm and prolific fancy of Praed are the gifts most fitted for the making of society verse. Here he comes as near greatness as the form will allow. The place in English literature of the author of *Quince*, *The Vicar* and *A Letter of Advice* is secure, though it is not among the highest.

The *vers de société* of Richard Monckton Milnes, Lord Houghton (1809—1885), deserves notice. But Milnes wrote gracefully upon so many other things that it is not easy to say in what he most excelled. Disraeli in *Tancred* has outlined his character in Mr Vavasour, and touched upon the "catholic sympathies and eclectic turn of mind" which enabled Milnes to see good in everything and everybody. It was this characteristic which impelled Carlyle to say to him, "There is only one post fit for you, and that is the office of perpetual president of the Heaven and Hell Amalgamation Society." Everyone loved Milnes; and W. E. Forster was the spokesman of all who knew the man when he said, "I have many friends who would be kind to me in distress, but only one who would be equally kind to me in disgrace." He befriended so many struggling authors that he came to be looked upon as the champion of the neglected man of letters. Milnes had great gifts and he was always "near something very glorious," but he never reached it. Perhaps the reason was the very readiness of his sympathy. He was attracted by Newmanism and pleaded for it in *One Tract More*; but when he went to the East he was equally ready to be pleased with Mahommedanism. In poetry, as in other things, Milnes was perhaps somewhat too versatile. He versified his travels, he competed with Macaulay and Aytoun in his *Poems, Legendary and Historical*, and he reached, perhaps, his highest point in the beautiful and pathetic lyric, *Strangers Yet*. But in nothing was he so uniformly successful as in *vers de société*.

In the religious verse of this period we see the deeply-marked influence of the Oxford Movement. That, naturally, inspires the poetry of Cardinal Newman, which has already been mentioned. It shows that, though he was surpassed by Keble in poetic achievement, in poetic *endowment* he ranked first among the promoters of the movement. But it was not in Newman only that this spirit was shown. In their degree it inspires minor writers such as Frederick William Faber, Isaac Williams and John Mason Neale. It inspires also a poet far greater than they—R. S. Hawker, author of *The Quest of the Sangraal*, and a spirited balladist as well. It was Hawker who, with *The Song of the Western Men*, deceived Scott, Macaulay and Dickens, all of whom believed it to be a genuine old ballad.

It is needless to dwell on the ambitious and immoderately long poem of *Festus*, by Philip James Bailey, a man who is sometimes regarded as the founder of the spasmodic school to be noticed later. There was a time when some good judges ranked *Festus* extraordinarily high, and it contains lines and passages of great merit. But it is fatally marred by the unpardonable style of the greater part of it. Neither is it necessary to do more than mention the political poets. *The Purgatory of Suicides*, by Thomas Cooper the Chartist, is notable rather because of the life of the author than for its poetic merit; and Capel Lofft's *Ernest, or Political Regeneration* has ceased to possess the power of curdling the blood which it exercised over our ancestors.

The Celtic poets must however be more seriously treated, were it only because they are one of the symptoms or phases of the great movement of nationality, which is a prominent feature in the history of the nineteenth century. This spirit generates a peculiarly local and also peculiarly intense form of patriotism, and patriotism is invariably accompanied by prejudice. The Englishman of the time of Napoleon was quite convinced that he was as good as three Frenchmen. In the same spirit the Celtic eulogists of Celtic writers have sometimes made their own geese swans. In reality, though we shall find an Irish flavour in much of the fiction of this period, we shall discover no Celtic novelist of the first rank; and though there were many Irish writers of verse there was no great Irish poet. Certainly George Darley, author of *Nepenthe* and *Sylvia*, cannot be called great; nor Trench, who is better known, and better deserves to be known, from his books on the English language than from his poetry. The one Celtic writer of this period who might even plausibly be called great was James Clarence Mangan (1803—1849), one of the numerous poets in whom great gifts have not been able to save their possessors from great misery. Some of Mangan's work is extremely fine—for example, *My Dark Rosaleen* and *The Karamanian Exile.* The latter is notable because it inspired the famous American poem, *Maryland, my Maryland*, and also because it is one of several instances of similarity between the work of Mangan and that of his American contemporary Poe.

There remain only the poetesses who come under this section. They have at least one thing in common with the Celtic poets. They are characteristic of the time by reason of their sex, as the others are by reason of race. Female writers of earlier days usually concealed their authorship as if it had been a crime. But sentiment changed, it ceased to be a questionable proceeding for women to write, and the natural result followed that far more of them did write. In the years just before the Victorian period Felicia Hemans and Letitia Elizabeth Landon were among the most popular writers of verse. A little later we find among the songstresses a daughter of Coleridge and no fewer than three of the daughters of Sheridan, one of whom, the celebrated Mrs Norton, is still well known for her *Bingen on the Rhine*. But three other women, Elizabeth Barrett Browning, Christina Rossetti, and Emily Brontë, overtopped all these. The two last will however be most conveniently noticed elsewhere.

Elizabeth Barrett (1806—1861), who by marriage became Elizabeth Browning, had been crippled by an accident at the age of fifteen, and lived, as she herself declares, a life as uneventful as that of a bird in a cage, until her union at forty with Robert Browning, a man six years her junior. In her childhood Mrs Browning gave evidence of unusual power. At the age of eight she read her Homer in the original. At a later date she studied Plato and all the Greek poets, and worked her way through the Bible in Hebrew. The friendship and love of Browning were of great value to her genius. They may almost be said to have awakened it. In her early days her poetic work was imitative, while part of her later work, written under the influence of her lover and husband, was singularly original. The *Sonnets from the Portuguese* are unique in English as the expression of the passion of love from the woman's point of view; for Christina Rossetti's *Monna Innominata* is inferior, and is moreover simply an effort of imagination, not a transcript of feeling; and Augusta Webster's exquisite sonnets *Mother and Daughter* deal with a love which, though no less sacred, is quite different. Of her own marriage Mrs Browning writes with a pen charged with emotion and a soul exalted by her love, yet humbled by her sense of unworthiness to be loved. No one else has ever given such poetic expression to this feeling from this standpoint.

The besetting sin of Mrs Browning is diffuseness. Her inability to condense has marred the charm and beauty of *The Cry of the Children*, *The Lay of the Brown Rosary*, *The Rhyme of the Duchess May* and *Lady Geraldine's Courtship*, as well as the verse romance of *Aurora Leigh*. The rigid law which limits the sonnet to fourteen lines was her salvation, and we can find no fault with such pieces as *A Soul's Expression*. *A Child's Grave at Florence*, though in a freer form, is also flawless. But diffuseness is a sin never wholly pardoned in literature, and especially in poetry; and therefore it is probable that, when the verdict of posterity is given, Mrs Browning's place will be less lofty than that which was given to her by her contemporaries.

§ 5. *The Turn of the Century*

By the year 1850 the three princes in the kingdom of letters, Carlyle, Tennyson and Browning, had fulfilled the high hopes they had awakened some twenty years earlier. They had all done work that the world would not willingly lose, and they were destined to do more. But from below a youthful band was climbing up. Among these there were no fewer than seven poets, some of them great, and all of considerable power. They were Edward FitzGerald, Matthew Arnold, Arthur Hugh Clough, Dante Gabriel Rossetti and his sister Christina Rossetti, Sydney Dobell and Alexander Smith. If we ask what were the forces that moulded these poets and the ideas that inspired their work, it will be found that the answer is threefold. They were influenced mainly by ideas of religion, by ideas of art, and by the sentiment of nationality. Clough and Arnold are the poets of the sceptical reaction against the teaching of Cardinal Newman and his friends. The Rossettis too were related to the Oxford Movement; but in their case the relation was one of sympathy, not of criticism, and in

Dante Rossetti the religious side was subordinate to the artistic one. FitzGerald stood alone, but he shows in the spirit of his work some kinship with the Oxford poets. Of the seven, Dobell exhibits most conspicuously the influence of the spirit of nationality. But it was present in others too, as was natural in view of the fact that 1848 was the year of the revolutions which shook every throne in Europe. Though the revolutionary movements were mostly unsuccessful, they produced momentous consequences, leading as they did to the partial disintegration of the Austrian empire and to the unification of Italy. The Chartist movement shows that England too was affected, though in a less degree. London was the asylum of hundreds of political refugees. Carlyle remembered seeing, at an earlier date, the "stately tragic figures" of exiled Spaniards; and the house of Dante Rossetti's father, himself a political refugee, was thronged with fellow-exiles from Italy. All this is naturally reflected in the poetry. We see its influence in the patriotic poems of Tennyson, in Mrs Browning's *Casa Guidi Windows*, but most conspicuously of all in the work of Sydney Dobell.

To Arthur Hugh Clough (1819—1861) and to Matthew Arnold (1822—1888) the questions of profoundest interest were questions of religion. They were both poets of doubt who would gladly have believed if they could, and each preaches the gospel of endurance and of work. Their early training as boys at Rugby School, under the father of Arnold, counts for much. There they learnt from the great head master to search for truth, and this teaching started in their minds the critical questioning which upset their faith in authority.

Clough was born in Liverpool, was taken to America when he was four, was brought back again five years later and sent to school at Rugby, which he left to become a scholar of Balliol College, Oxford. After taking his degree he was elected a fellow, and afterwards a tutor, of Oriel College; but he resigned both these posts when he was twenty-nine, because he felt that his position gave him the appearance of believing many things which he did not believe. His friends were dismayed at his decision, for it was not clear how he was to earn his daily bread. Clough was however almost at once invited to become head of University Hall, London, which was a place of residence for students. The few months between the date of his appointment and the commencement of his duties were spent in Italy. He was in Rome during its siege by the French, and there he wrote *Amours de Voyage*, a correspondence in verse. It was not published till 1858. After a short time he resigned his appointment in University Hall and went to America with the intention of settling there. He was however recalled to a position in the Education Office in London, in which he spent the few years that remained to him of life, too busy to write much poetry.

The Bothie of Tober-na-Vuolich was not Clough's first poem, but it was the first in order of publication. It appeared after he had come to the end of what he calls his "spiritual servitude as a teacher of the thirty-nine articles." It is like the work of a prisoner suddenly set at liberty, and is full of the jests and high spirits of the schoolboy at recess. His most ambitious work is *Dipsychus*, which was not published in his lifetime. It too closely resembles Goethe's *Faust*, and suffers from the inevitable comparison. Perhaps the most interesting thing to notice about the poem is the presence in it of the remarkable conception that good may be evolved not only out of physical evil, but even out of sin. This is a favourite thought of the nineteenth century. It is reiterated again and again by Browning, and it is the very soul and substance of Nathaniel Hawthorne's great romance, *The Marble Faun*. So in Clough we read,

> "What we call sin
> I could believe a painful opening out
> Of paths for ampler virtue."

Clough loves best to move in the region of such profound ethical and religious ideas. They are present in the best of his shorter poems too, for example, in *Easter Day* and *The New Sinai.*

Matthew Arnold followed his friend to Oxford four years later, and, like him, disappointed his tutors by taking a second class. But his place in the honours list had not hidden his real power from his contemporaries. J. C. Shairp, the critic and poet, describes Arnold at this time as

> "So full of power, yet blithe and debonair,
> Rallying his friends with pleasant banter gay,
> Or half-a-dream chaunting with jaunty air
> Great words of Goethe, catch of Béranger."

The fellows of Oriel likewise recognised his power, and gave him a fellowship; and Lord Lansdowne soon afterwards made him his private secretary. At the age of twenty-nine he became an inspector of schools, in which position he remained almost to the end of his life. But for ten years he held also the more congenial office of professor of poetry at Oxford, and to his tenure of this chair we owe the valuable lectures *On Translating Homer.*

Arnold's poetry was chiefly the product of his early life. His first volume was *The Strayed Reveller*; three years later came *Empedocles on Etna*; then a volume of *Poems,* partly new and partly old. *Thyrsis* (1866), an exquisite elegy on the death of his friend Clough, and *New Poems* (1867) are almost the last of Arnold's poetical works. Afterwards he wrote only a few fugitive pieces suggested by passing events. Such are the elegy on the death of Dean Stanley and the beautiful verses in memory of the dead pets, the dogs Geist and Kaiser and the canary Matthias, which are buried in the garden of his home at Cobham.

When *The Strayed Reveller* was published Arnold was considerably older in years than Browning and Tennyson when they first appeared as poets. Unlike them in mental development, he had nearly reached his full stature in poetry. The whole period of his poetic activity was less than twenty years, and there was no line dividing the verse of his youth from the finished product of his maturer years. In the contents of this first book of poems we find the circle of Arnold's thoughts and interests almost complete. There is omitted from it only one type which he afterwards wrote, and wrote finely—the narrative in blank verse; for, though there is no elegy, in *Resignation*, in *The Sick King of Bokhara* and *To a Gipsy Child* there is plenty of the elegiac spirit. It is true we could ill spare what in the later volumes he gives us, but the themes he chooses are not wholly new. The same thoughts are reiterated with fresh illustrations. Arnold felt that there was much amiss in the world, and his verse is tinged with melancholy. In his own words, for him, as for the author of *Obermann*, all through nature

> "There sobs I know not what ground-tone
> Of human agony."

The poet had little faith in his own generation, because it seemed to him to have flung off the duties and high ideals of the past. The old world was dead and the new "powerless to be born." The gloom is occasionally mistaken for affectation, and for this reason the poetry of Arnold is by some actively disliked: it is certainly misunderstood. But for Arnold to put by this gloom would have been equivalent to putting by his own nature. Perhaps he holds himself too much aloof from the rush and hurry of modern life; for many feel that his poetry is passionless, cold, "like a starry night with a touch of frost—beautiful and chilly." There is no movement in his half-dramatic poem *Empedocles on Etna* or in the narratives *Balder Dead* and *Sohrab and Rustum.*

In all his works there is no passionate outburst, no red-hot emotion. Everything is restrained: in his own words we must "possess our souls." "A criticism of life" is the definition Arnold gives of poetry, and this best explains the spirit in which he wrote. His model was classic, and the human forces of modern England were alien to his ideal. Swinburne understood the value of Arnold's verse when he spoke of the "absolute loveliness of sound and colour" in the song of Callicles in *Empedocles on Etna.* It is the same perfection which delights us in *Requiescat.* Arnold lived near, but he shrank from, the "sick hurry" of modern life, its "divided aims." For that reason he could never, any more than his contemporary Edward FitzGerald, be the poet of the people as Tennyson was.

Arnold was in the world, but not of it. FitzGerald was neither in it nor of it. His life was spent in such retirement that in writing to Carlyle eight months after the death of Mrs Carlyle, he sent her his compliments. His letters and his verses are the work of a born man of letters, and his prose dialogue *Euphranor* is in exquisite English. But his greatest achievement is the translation of the Persian poet, Omar Khayyám, who lived eight hundred years ago and left behind him in his verse a record of his philosophy of life. He bids us "eat, drink and be merry, for to-morrow we die." This is an injunction which hardly commends itself to us by either its novelty or its morality. But behind it there is a deeper meaning in Omar—what Matthew Arnold calls "the infinite regret for all that might have been." It is curious to notice the resemblance between the Latin poet Horace and the translation of FitzGerald. Horace is purely of the western world, but the English Omar is a blend of Oriental voluptuousness with the restraint of the Roman stoic; and although the original quatrains were written in a far-off country and in a far-away time, the *Rubáiyát*, as reinterpreted by FitzGerald, are a criticism of a life which men are living here and now.

Of the first edition of FitzGerald's great work only two hundred and fifty copies were printed, and two hundred of these were given to Quaritch the bookseller, who sold them at one penny each. Rossetti and Swinburne bought theirs at this price. Now, a small library has grown up around the 404 lines of FitzGerald's *Omar Khayyám*. Although it professes to be only a translation, it is, as Professor Norton says, "the work of a poet inspired by a poet; not a copy but a reproduction, not a translation but the redelivery of a poetic inspiration."

The next great poet of the seven who appeared at this period is Dante Gabriel Rossetti (1828—1882). He was the son of Italian parents, born and brought up in England, where his father had taken refuge because of political opinions which were held to be treasonable in his native country. But though Rossetti was by blood three-quarters Italian, his brother says "he liked England and the English better than any other country or nation," and his mind was moulded on its literature. He was a painter as well as a poet, and was the leading spirit of the famous Pre-Raphaelite Brotherhood, who about this time revolted against "the contemptible and even scandalous condition of British art." The first pictures inspired by their ideals were exhibited in the galleries of 1849; and the first writings which expressed their new conceptions of art were printed in a magazine called *The Germ* which appeared and disappeared in the early months of 1850. It did not pay, and the contributors were too poor to maintain it longer.

In 1860 Rossetti married Elizabeth Siddal, whose face looks out at us from many of his pictures. In less than two years she died from an overdose of laudanum, a drug she was in the habit of taking to soothe her nerves. In his grief Rossetti buried the MSS of his poems in her coffin; but about seven years later the grave was opened and the poems were recovered. In 1861 *The Early Italian Poets*, afterwards entitled *Dante and His Circle*, had appeared. It was however by the poems reclaimed from the tomb and published in 1870 that Rossetti first became widely known to English readers, and it is on these and on the *Ballads and Sonnets* of 1881 that his fame in literature will chiefly depend. But a great mistake would be made if we were to date Rossetti's influence from 1870. Ruskin was right in pronouncing him to be "the chief intellectual force in the establishment of the Modern Romantic School in England"; and the Modern Romantic School dates from about 1850. The explanation is that Rossetti had contributed both poetry and prose to *The Germ* and to *The Oxford and Cambridge Magazine*, and these contributions, as well as other poems which remained in MS, were well known to a small body of highly-gifted men, including, among others, William Morris, Swinburne and Burne Jones. Besides, Rossetti had another means of expression in the art of painting. Thus he was moulding literature and art for at least twenty years before the publication of his earliest volume of original verse.

What struck contemporaries most powerfully in the volume of 1870 was the rich sensuousness of the verse. In imparting this quality to his poems Rossetti had the high authority of Milton, who declared that poetry ought to be sensuous as well as simple and impassioned. But the sensuous easily passes into the sensual, or may be mistaken for it. Sometimes, perhaps, the border line was passed by Rossetti; and Robert Buchanan, one of his critics, fell into the mistake of believing that the transition was made and the line passed habitually. He attacked Rossetti in an article entitled *The Fleshly School of Poetry*; and, though he afterwards repented and recanted, it was not so easy to annul the effect of his bitter words. Buchanan was certainly wrong, but he was not wholly without excuse. Some of Rossetti's poems are luscious in the extreme. Beautiful as are the sonnets of *The House of Life* individually, they form, when taken together as a whole, a poem whose effect is not bracing, but enervating. They cloy with sweetness. Yet on the other hand there are both sonnets and other poems by Rossetti whose tone is in the highest degree heroic. Such, among the sonnets, are *Thomas Chatterton*, *The Last Three from Trafalgar*, and, perhaps greatest of all, the noble *Lost Days*.

It is strange that, artist though he was and devotee of the religion of beauty, Rossetti occasionally fell into the worst errors of taste. He sometimes stooped to what must be pronounced no better than literary trickery, and he affords here and there examples of the most objectionable sort of "poetic diction." "The smooth black stream that makes thy whiteness fair" are the words in which he describes the ink used to write a love-letter; and there was never any poetic periphrasis, even in the eighteenth century, more absurd.

In his later work, which is embodied in the *Ballads and Sonnets* of 1881, although his mind was disturbed by drugs and his character distorted by suspicion and distrust of his best friends, Rossetti's inspiration did not fail. But it somewhat changed its character. In the earlier poetry there was little or no narrative, while the later collection includes a number of well-told stories. *The White Ship* is a ballad of the tragic death of the children of Henry I, and *The King's Tragedy* is a story of James I of Scotland. No attempt is made to imitate the genuine popular ballad. These pieces are frankly modern and are unmistakably the product of a sophisticated age. But as narratives they are as effective as the old ballads themselves. In the later volume there is a larger proportion than in the earlier of poems which might be described as virile, and there is far less excuse for such an attack as that which Robert Buchanan had made.

In some ways we shall understand Dante Rossetti better when we have followed the working of the same spirit in his gifted sister Christina Rossetti (1830—1894). Though both were influenced by the Oxford Movement, its influence on Christina was far deeper than its influence on Dante Rossetti. To her the Church of the middle ages, with all its ordinances and its ceremonies, was a reality, and her worship of it the moving force of her life. Her poems are chiefly devotional. The mystery of death and the sadness of life are ever before her mind. Renunciation and resignation are the notes she loves. Her sonnet-sequence, *Monna Innominata*, treats of love which ends unhappily; in *Looking Forward* she asks for "poppies brimmed with sleepy death"; in *The Convent Threshold* and *Amor Mundi* she writes of the smoothness of the path of sin and the difficulty of reform. Her melancholy *Despised and Rejected* ends with the despairing moan,

> "And on my door
> The mark of blood for evermore."

There is monotony in her melancholy, but her sincerity is impressive. Not all her work however is in grey shadows. *Goblin Market*, *No, thank you, John*, and *The Prince's Progress*, though the last ends sadly, have cheerful touches, and they show much of the delicate purity and simplicity of her mind. And if in some of her religious verse there is a gloom due to the sense of sin, elsewhere there is an exultation which has caused certain of her pieces to be described as "the national hymns of Heaven."

Christina Rossetti stands in contrast to her brother at all points. He is sensuous and gorgeous while her verse is refined and simple. She stands straining her eyes towards heaven, while he makes the Blessed Damozel gaze back with yearning from heaven to earth. To him the Oxford Movement meant a revival of colour and beauty, to her it meant greater opportunity for sacrifice and suffering. Her attitude was that of Newman. Her brother found in the middle ages merely material for the art that was his religion.

Another writer of this group is Coventry Patmore (1823—1896), but in his faith he is nearer to Christina than to Dante Rossetti. Patmore's fluency in writing has led both himself and his critics astray. His poem, *The Angel in the House*, was to celebrate wedded love; and he boasted that here he, the latest of poets, had found "the first of themes." A less self-confident man would have paused before pronouncing a subject never sung before "the first of themes." Patmore had no misgivings. But the first part did not get beyond *The Betrothal*; *The Espousals* ended the second part; and after *Faithful for Ever* there is silence until three years later, when there was a sequel, *The Victories of Love*. The whole work tended to show that "the first of themes" is in reality ill suited for poetry. Patmore used up many precious years in this attempt. He probably became conscious of the mistake he had made, for his *Odes* and his greatest poem *Amelia* are as unlike as possible to his first scheme.

Contemporary with Patmore was Sydney Dobell (1824—1874), the chief of the spasmodic poets, whose grandfather, Samuel Thompson, had founded the religious sect known to its own congregations as the Church of God, but called by outsiders the sect of Free-thinking Christians. The founder had the unusual experience of being cast out from the church of his own creation. But his grandson, Sydney Dobell, was recognised as the child born to be the guiding star and chief priest of the community. There was no school or university in England fit to be trusted with the training of the future leader of "the Church of God." It is a remarkable proof of Dobell's mental vitality and strength of character that, in spite of all this unwholesome worship and adulation, he lost little except the power of self-criticism. His life was probably shortened, and his health and nerves certainly suffered, by the strain of excitement and religious emotion. Ultimately he grew out of "the Church of God," and shook himself free from its teaching. An interest in European politics filled the vacant place. It was a time of wide-spread unrest, and Dobell's imagination was stirred by the revolt of Hungary and Italy. His poem *The Roman* was like a trumpet-call to the political exiles, and it drew together at the poet's home at Coxhorne "the Society of the Friends of Italy." Dobell's later poems, *The Magyar's New-Year-Eve*, and *The Youth of England to Garibaldi's Legion*, are also inspired by the rising of the nations against the tyranny of kings and popes.

His second poem, *Balder*, is a work of vast design. He proposed in the preface "to treat of the progress of a Human Being from Doubt to Faith, from Chaos to Order." But his design was never accomplished, only the first of the three parts of which it was to consist having ever been written. The poem has been likened to Ibsen's *Brand*, and it has points of resemblance to Browning's *Paracelsus* also. It was not well received. Dobell however was indifferent to criticism, and he unfortunately believed that "poetry should roll from the heart as tears from the eye unbidden." Hence he never checked the flow, and rarely revised what he had written.

It was W. E. Aytoun who applied to the group of which Dobell was chief the witty nickname of the Spasmodic School. Another member of it was Alexander Smith (1829—1867), the son of a pattern-designer, who, after a boyhood and youth of poverty and difficulty, won at twenty-four a sudden and brilliant success with a volume of *Poems*. He followed this up with *City Poems* four years later, in which he showed still higher ability. But the reaction had come, and Smith was punished for over-praise in the first instance, for which he was in no way responsible, by subsequent neglect and depreciation. This led him in the latter part of his life to prefer prose to verse. He has written both with great charm, and, in spite of neglect, he is a true, and in a few pieces almost a great poet. The piece entitled *Glasgow* is one of the finest ever dedicated to a British city, and the lyric *Barbara* well deserves a place in our anthologies. So too for the sake of some paragraphs in *A Lark's Flight*, one of the essays in the prose volume entitled *Dreamthorp*, he deserves a place among the masters of English prose.

§ 6. *The Later Pre-Raphaelites*

Contemporary with the Pre-Raphaelites of the last chapter and one of the intimate friends of Rossetti was William Morris (1834—1896). He was the son of a man of means and received the usual education of an English gentleman. Marlborough was his school and Oxford his university. At the latter he met Burne Jones the artist. Both men intended to become clergymen, but art drew them away from the Church. They were attracted by the ideals of the Pre-Raphaelites, whose enthusiasm for the beauties of mediævalism Morris shared. He was a man who played many parts in life, and when he calls himself "the idle singer of an empty day" he does less than justice to himself. His biographer, quoting from the *Fasti Britannici*, sums him up as "Poet, artist, manufacturer, and socialist, author of *The Earthly Paradise*," and adds that in this terse, unimpassioned entry we find a description which Morris would himself have accepted as substantially accurate. We are chiefly concerned with the literary side of Morris, but it is interesting to recall how he came to turn his mind to the making of furniture. When he married and wanted to build and furnish a house, the impossibility of finding for money anything but ugliness was driven home to him, and this experience led to the formation of the firm of Morris & Co. He was the guiding genius, the artist who chose the colours and designed the papers for walls and the curtains and all the other forms of house decoration which came to push aside the hideous fashions of the time. The practical knowledge of industry thus acquired opened his eyes to the want of beauty and lack of comfort in the lives of the working classes, on whose behalf he, of all the writers of the time, was the most strenuous labourer. The thirteenth century, although he saw its imperfections, had for him the ideal workshops; for then every labourer was an artist and took pleasure in the beautiful objects he made. Morris would have reproduced this in the nineteenth century. It was not his plan to push men out of the industrial ranks in which they were born and move them up to a higher social class—the only true reform, he held, was for each class to keep its best members in it. In the guilds of the middle ages he thought he saw the proper recognition of knowledge and merit and the proper organisation for the protection of the workmen and the maintenance of the quality of their work.

Morris's writings, like his practical work, drew inspiration from another time and also from another land than his own. In his early life we have the Arthurian poem *The Defence of Guenevere*, which has far more of the real spirit of its period than Tennyson's *Idylls of the King*; later, in *The Life and Death of Jason* and in *The Earthly Paradise*, there is much of the spirit of Chaucer. The last-named is a great collection of stories. The plan is similar to that pursued in *The Canterbury Tales*, but we miss the spirited narrative and the humour of its fourteenth century model. There are 42,000 lines in it, and neither the length nor the dreamy tone of the poem accords with the character of an active practical man of affairs, such as Morris showed himself in the business of life.

After Chaucer, Morris found interest in almost none of the writers of the Italian Renascence or the Elizabethans, and hardly any of the poetry between them and the revival of romance appealed to him. But his love of the mystical and of the vague dreaminess of mediæval romance did not prevent him from developing enthusiasm for the simple direct epic poetry of the Scandinavian poets. Carlyle in his *Heroes and Hero-Worship* had already turned the attention of Englishmen to the poetry of the Norsemen and had pointed out how closely it was related to ourselves. *The Lovers of Gudrun* was written before Morris had been to Iceland. He went there in 1871 and then again in 1873, and was much more delighted with the land to which the northern Sagas belong than with Italy, which he visited in the time between his two northern journeys. The outcome of the enthusiasm aroused by these two pilgrimages was the northern epic *Sigurd the Volsung*, his finest piece. In this the narrative is spirited and beautiful, and it has none of the monotony of the mediæval stories of Morris.

Sigurd the Volsung was the last of Morris's long poems. He had previously tried his hand at mediæval drama in the morality play of *Love is Enough; or the Freeing of Pharamond*; and though it was a failure, *Sir Peter Harpdon's End* proves that he had some dramatic instinct. One of the most impressive of the characteristics of Morris is that he is more at home in the distant ages which he recreated by his imagination, and in alien countries, than in his own. His whole life is an effort to bring back the spirit that is dead, not to copy it but to make it live again;

and at this point his manifold work as artist, manufacturer, socialist, and poet finds unity. "Time was," he says, "when everybody that made anything made a work of art besides a useful piece of goods, *and it gave them pleasure to make it.*"

Though Algernon Charles Swinburne (1837—1909) was only three years younger than Morris, he seems to belong to a time much nearer to-day than Morris or their other friend Burne Jones. He was educated at Eton and at Balliol College, Oxford. Lady Burne Jones gives a striking and attractive description of Swinburne in his youth. "His appearance was very unusual and in some ways beautiful, for his hair was glorious in abundance and colour, and his eye indescribably fine.......He was restless beyond words, scarcely standing still at all, and almost dancing as he walked, while even in sitting he moved continually, seeming to keep time by a swift movement of the hands at the wrists and sometimes of the feet also, with some inner rhythm of excitement. He was courteous and affectionate and unsuspicious, and faithful beyond most people to those he really loved. The biting wit which filled his talk so as at times to leave his hearers dumb with amazement always spared one thing, and that was an absent friend."

The first book published by Swinburne, *The Queen Mother: Rosamond*, appeared when he was twenty-three. It passed unnoticed, but *Atalanta in Calydon*, his next work, which came out five years later, had a very different reception. Tennyson shook his head over it and said cold things, Browning frankly said it was "a fuzz of words"; but the majority of critics felt that since the days of Milton no such drama in classic form had appeared. The melody of the verse and the variety of the word-music opened the eyes of the world to the capacities of the English language for lyric measures, and the youth of the singer led men to form high hopes for the work that was to come. A half-playful wildness led him in his later publication, *Poems and Ballads*, to print some objectionable verses. Public opinion was shocked, and Moxon, the publisher, would have nothing more to do with Swinburne. Besides the obnoxious pieces there were some very beautiful poems in this collection, which were passed over unnoticed in the storm of abuse visited upon the objectionable verses.

Swinburne's work may be classified in two chief divisions—the dramas and the poems, the latter being chiefly lyrical. In his youth his great desire was to be a dramatist, and in the dedicatory epistle prefixed to the collected poems he avows that his strongest ambition is "to do something worth doing, and not utterly unworthy of a young countryman of Marlowe the teacher and Webster the pupil of Shakespeare, in the line of work which those three poets had left as a possibly unattainable example for ambitious Englishmen." It proved unattainable by Swinburne. *Atalanta in Calydon* owed its success to its Greek setting and to the ringing music of its choruses; and the three dramatic versions of the romance of Mary Queen of Scots, *Chastelard*, *Bothwell* and *Mary Stuart*, won little or no appreciation from the critics. But Swinburne still regarded the drama as the highest form of creative art, and he could not believe that his powers were not equal to its production. His next attempt was *Marino Faliero*, then came *Locrine* and *Rosamund, Queen of the Lombards*. All this work suffers from want of restraint. No audience can be found willing to listen to actors delivering speeches hundreds of lines long.

The great glory of Swinburne's poetry is its music. His verse came without effort and ran on as easily as of the song of a bird in the bush. It is even too facile, and this excessive facility is the point of H. D. Traill's delightful parody, in which an amazed world asks, "Master, how is it done?" and the poet answers:

"Let this thing serve you to know:
When the river of rhymes should flow
I turn on the tap, and they come."

The two long poems, *Tristram of Lyonesse* and *The Tale of Balin*, are interesting as attempts to re-tell the mediæval tales with more fidelity to the spirit of the originals than had been shown by Tennyson. Here and there they are highly poetical. But they are interesting also because they confirm the impression left by the dramas that the genius of Swinburne was essentially lyrical. As wholes they are unsatisfactory, for the poet had not in great measure the gift of narrative, any more than he had the gift of dramatic conception and construction.

Swinburne, like Byron and Shelley, was the champion of the distressed, the poet of liberty. The struggle of Italy for freedom, the oppressive tyranny the Russian nobles exercised over their serfs, neglected genius, unrecognised merit, all stirred him profoundly. The Hungarian patriot, Louis Kossuth, is celebrated in one of the finest of English sonnets because, as Swinburne says,

"His hand is raised to smite
Men's heads abased before the Muscovite."

Yet he was an enthusiastic and hopeful imperialist, and since the death of Tennyson there has been no poet so patriotic as Swinburne. His verse is filled with the imperialism which longs "to keep our noble England whole"—a republican England he had in his mind, the country ruled by Cromwell, not by Victoria.

Swinburne wrote prose as well as verse, and for natural gifts of criticism he was unsurpassed. But unfortunately his want of self-restraint told more seriously against him here than in his poetry. His panegyrics are unmeasured, he seems to know no degree of comparison but the superlative. Again and again however—for example in the cases of Blake and of FitzGerald—he did invaluable service to genius unrecognised.

Perhaps John Byrne Leicester Warren, Lord de Tabley (1835—1895), may also, though with some reserve, be classed with the later Pre-Raphaelites. Though he was senior to Swinburne he was powerfully influenced by the younger man, and through him by Rossetti. He was a man with many interests, who attained a certain mastery in all he tried. In botany and in the sciences that treat of coins and shells, as well as in all that relates to books, his learning was wide and deep. Yet his unusual knowledge did not make Warren a pedant, and although his poetry contains allusions to a great variety of birds and flowers, there is always a pictorial reason for their place in his verse. His mind developed late. His earliest volumes contain little that is worthy of remembrance. It was not until he published *Rehearsals* and *Searching the Net*, many years after he had begun to write, that his genius came into full flower. In the interval however he had written *Philoctetes* and *Orestes*, the finest dramas of the classical type, except Swinburne's, in our recent literature. He was never popular. Interest was aroused for a moment, after many years of indifference, by the republication of a selection of his best pieces under the title *Poems*, *Dramatic and Lyric*. But the interest soon subsided; a second series was received with comparative coldness; and the poet, now Lord de Tabley, died disappointed.

Lord de Tabley, though a strong and original poet, was very sensitive to the human influences with which he came in touch. Perhaps, as has already been suggested, the most obvious is the influence of the Pre-Raphaelites, which is seen in such poems as the *Hymn to Astarte*; but he himself declared that Tennyson appealed to him, both in his early and in his later life, more than any other poet;

and the marks of Tennyson's influence are visible to every student. Then again, both in form and in substance some of his finest pieces bear the stamp of Browning. There is certainly something of Browning in the masterly dramatic monologue of *Jael*, which many think the finest thing De Tabley ever wrote. But if De Tabley took hints, even as Shakespeare did, like Shakespeare also he invariably added the incommunicable something of his own which proclaims the true poet. In our recent literary history there are few things more to be regretted than the fact that neglect and lack of appreciation chilled and silenced him.

§ 7. *The Celtic Poets*

It has been necessary in an earlier part to notice that Celticism which is one phase of the remarkable growth of national spirit characteristic of the nineteenth century. This Celtic revival went on contemporaneously with the Pre-Raphaelite movement and was intimately associated with it. Burne Jones the painter and William Morris both came of Welsh blood. The latter however was Teutonic rather than Celtic in sentiment, and it was the Scandinavian, not the Welsh race he selected for glorification. Sir Lewis Morris (1833—1907), also a Welshman, turned for inspiration to another world and gained great popularity by his treatment of it. His *Epic of Hades* has gone through forty editions. His *Songs of two Worlds*, *Songs Unsung* and *Songs of Britain* have also been bought and read by thousands. But his work is not of high merit, and his facility in verse-making lowered his standard.

Arthur O'Shaughnessy (1844—1881) and Aubrey de Vere (1814—1902), son of the dramatist already noticed, are two Celts from Ireland. O'Shaughnessy was a man of sensitive poetic temperament who embodied a little of Swinburne, a little of Rossetti and a little of William

Morris in his work, imitating unfortunately their faults rather than their graces. De Vere was Celtic by birth, but his poetry recalls Wordsworth too much to be in any sense typical of the race. He has several volumes treating of a great variety of subjects, and some of these belong to Ireland—*The Sisters*, *Inisfail and other Poems*, *The Legends of St Patrick*, and *The Foray of Queen Meave.* He has written dramas too—*Alexander the Great* and *St Thomas of Canterbury.* But everywhere he is too diffuse and sometimes he is obscure to his reader, as possibly he was to himself.

Perhaps the most imposing figure among the Celts is Robert Buchanan (1841—1901), who combined in his own person the blood of Scotland, Wales and England. Though born in England, he was the most Scottish of all our recent poets. Even in many of his poems in pure English we recognise the northern landmarks. The scenery, the sailors, the peasants, the shepherds, their mothers, wives and sisters have all the characteristics of the folk who live north of the Tweed, or at any rate north of the Humber. Such scenes and such characters fill *Idyls and Legends of Inverburn* and *North Coast Poems*; and in these we see one aspect of the poet. We see another in *London Poems.* Their realism is powerful indeed, but less beautiful than that of the poems of the North Country; yet even in the *London Poems* we are lit and warmed by gleams of imagination that transfigure the realism.

Buchanan's father was a Glasgow journalist, a sceptic and a follower of Robert Owen the socialist. The boy's religious experiences were not ordinary. He was brought up without biblical instruction, and it was not until he reached manhood that he became familiar with the creeds of the Churches. He never acquired any definite faith, but he tried to make himself sympathise with the Christian point of view. *The City of Dream*, an allegory dedicated "to the sainted spirit" of John Bunyan, gives a picture of Buchanan's confused search for a heavenly kingdom. *The Wandering Jew*, another poem of this class, gives an original and impressive description of a Christ grown old, grey and weary; a Christ who is bowed and broken by the wicked deeds which his followers have done in his name. This poem was "his favourite child." He began it in 1866, kept it by him for thirty-three years, and published it near the end of his life. But many critics regard *The Book of Orm* as Buchanan's highest flight. Here he puts off realism and appears in the character of a mystic, because he considers that mysticism is the peculiar gift of the Celt, to whom he dedicates the poem. The work was too ambitious, and Buchanan was hardly profound enough to deal with a subject so difficult. It is a long jump from this solemn poem to the rollicking laughter of *The Wedding of Shon Maclean* and Buchanan's other humorous pieces. Except Mr Rudyard Kipling no recent poet has shown such a great gift of humour as Buchanan; nor is there any one who has given examples of powerful work in so many different ways. Had he been able to fuse the elements of his greatness, his place in literature would be in the company of the giants.

§ 8. *The remaining Poets*

Not only have the poets of the nineteenth century expressed almost every shade of belief and unbelief, but even the misery of blank despair has found a singer in James Thomson (1834—1882). He began his life and ended it in misfortune. His father was stricken with paralysis when the boy was six years old, and the duty of providing for the home fell upon the mother, "a deeply religious woman of the Irvingite faith, whose nature, unlike that of her husband, seems to have been of a melancholy cast." Possibly Thomson inherited his pessimism from her. Some however trace it to the death of a beautiful girl with whom he was in love. In Ireland he met the politician Charles Bradlaugh, who became his best friend. Thomson at a later date wrote some of his finest pieces as contributions to Bradlaugh's paper, *The National Reformer*. His greatest poem, *The City of Dreadful Night*, is probably the gloomiest in the language, though *Insomnia* rivals it. But Thomson could be bright and genial as well as gloomy, and this lighter mood finds expression in *The Lord of the Castle of Indolence*, and those *Idylls of Cockaigne*, *Sunday up the River* and *Sunday at Hampstead*. Even near the end of his life he remained capable of mirth. When he had quarrelled with his patron Bradlaugh and cut himself adrift from the means of living, Thomson suddenly burst into the bright and beautiful verses *Richard Forest's Midsummer Night*, *He heard her Sing* and *At Belvoir*. But this was the last flash before the darkness. On June 3rd of the same year 1882, after four terrible weeks of "intemperance, homelessness, and desperation," this gifted poet died in University College Hospital, London, whither he had been carried from the home of his blind friend, the poet Philip Bourke Marston.

Contemporary with Buchanan and Thomson there was a small group of women singers who each left good work. Adelaide Procter (1825—1864), the gifted "elf-child" of the poet Barry Cornwall, has left behind her verses which Charles Dickens praised and accepted for his *Household Words*. Her *Legends and Lyrics* were more in demand ten years after the death of their author than the poetry of any writer then living except Tennyson. But in spite of this popularity Adelaide Procter never wrote verse of the same high order and strength as that which we find in *High Tide on the Coast of Lincolnshire* by Jean Ingelow (1820—1897), whose *Poems*, published in 1863, ran into a fourth edition before the close of the year. Her *Echo and the Ferry*, *Requiescat in Pace* and *Divided* are fine pieces. Though she is not a great poet, it is not too much to say that, among women poets, she is surpassed only by Mrs Browning, Christina Rossetti, Emily Brontë and Augusta Webster (1837—1894).

Mrs Webster's work is little known, but for sheer strength her only rival in this group is Emily Brontë. So great is she, indeed, that some of those who have studied her think that to her, rather than to Mrs Browning or to Christina Rossetti, ought to be assigned the primacy among English poetesses, and an able critic has even pronounced her drama *The Sentence* to be "one of the masterpieces of European drama." But Mrs Webster's most characteristic, and perhaps, notwithstanding this opinion, her best work, is to be found in the dramatic monologues of the collections entitled *Dramatic Studies* and *Portraits*. She was influenced by Browning, and the best of her monologues are worthy of comparison even with his.

There remain four poets who lived at this time, and who cannot be linked with each other or classed with any other group, though they may have special relations with one or other of their contemporaries. Thus William Ernest Henley (1849—1903) was associated with R. L. Stevenson in the writing of plays; and our first picture of the poet comes from the pen of Stevenson, who visited him when he was a patient in an Edinburgh hospital, and found him "sitting up in bed with his hair and beard all tangled, and talking as cheerfully as if he had been in a king's palace, or the great King's palace of the blue air." The long months passed on this sickbed not only found for Henley a friend, but also gave him a subject for his poems, *In Hospital*. A publisher was harder to come by. The poet says that these verses were rejected by every editor of standing in London. The editors were wrong;

yet the fact that afterwards three magazines failed under his direction shows that in the commercial sense Henley was somewhat dangerous. He was daring, forceful and original. But he had not the gift of the story-teller, and it is not certain that without aid he could have written plays. Given a subject like the hospital however, or the streets of London, or the glory of his country, Henley could write splendid verse.

Manly, vigorous, simple-hearted, original, Henley forms a striking contrast to Owen Meredith, the *nom de guerre* of the second Lord Lytton (1831—1891). Lytton had little originality of mind, and his work is a mirror which reflects the society in which he moved. His genius was so receptive that there is scarcely a contemporary of note of whom echoes may not be found in his verse. He was not a mere copyist, but his mind, like the clear surface of still water, reflected every shadow that crossed it. *Clytemnestra* was the first of a series of volumes of poetry which, in spite of high office as Viceroy of India and Ambassador of England in Paris, he contrived to make tolerably long. He was among the most popular poets of his time; but during the last generation his fame has greatly declined.

One of the characteristics of the later Victorian era was a growing interest in the literature of the East. In *Serbski Pesme* Lytton made a contribution to this interest. But Edwin Arnold (1832—1904) looked farther East, and made the satisfaction of this interest his principal literary task. He became famous through his poetic rendering of Buddhism. *The Light of Asia*, a long poem on this theme, delighted the people of England, who were eager to learn what there was to be told about a religion older than their own. Arnold tried afterwards in other poems to do for the religion of Christ and for the faith of Mahomet what he had done for Buddhism, but in both these efforts he failed to hit the public taste.

Far more highly gifted than Edwin Arnold was Francis

Thompson (1859—1907). His most famous poem is *The Hound of Heaven*, and the opening verses are worthy of a place among the grandest lyrics. But unfortunately Thompson was not quite sure in his touch even in *The Hound of Heaven*, and in some of his other pieces his lapses into bad taste are scarcely credible. Had he lived longer the dross might have been burned and purged away. As it is, we can only say that he was a man who at times wrote nobly, but also at times deplorably ill. His usual style is grand and sonorous almost to excess, but occasionally he writes with a charming simplicity, as for example in the exquisite Wordsworthian piece *Daisy*.

It is perhaps a chronological error to place George Meredith (1828—1909) at the end of the chapter on poets and poetesses. But his span of productive life stretched for nearly fifty years, and if we place him near the author of *In Memoriam* or *The Strayed Reveller*, where he stands by the date of his first poem *Chillianwallah* (1849), we are at fault with *A Reading of Life* (1901). The grandson and son of tailors, Meredith was born at Portsmouth (the Lymport of *Evan Harrington*) and educated in a Moravian school in Germany. At the age of twenty-one he began to study law, cultivating it very literally on a little oatmeal; for his daily fare was one bowl of porridge. In the same eventful year he published his first piece, *Chillianwallah*, in *Chambers's Journal*, and also married the flippant Mary Ellen, a daughter of the novelist Thomas Love Peacock. It was impossible to keep a house on the first elements of law, so he left the office and settled down near his father-in-law to labour at journalism, doing this work, in his own words, "with his toes, to leave room for serener occupations above." His wife left him, and he and his little son lived together in great frugality, the father, as he said, "laying traps for money." At one time he was reader to the publishers Chapman and Hall, and he lost them much money by refusing to accept *East Lynne*, *The Heavenly Twins* and other novels destined to catch the passing fancy, as well as Butler's *Erewhon*. He was also on the staff of *The Morning Post* and was sent out by his helpful friend Algernon Borthwick as special correspondent with the Italian forces towards the end of their war against Austria. So the struggle went on until late in life, when he was left a small legacy which gave him pecuniary independence and set him free to write what he liked.

Meredith's poetry is sufficient in bulk as well as in quality to give reasonable support to the contention of those admirers who maintain that he is a poet in the first place and a novelist in the second. It is within the limits of possibility that his poetry may become better known than his prose. As poet he is unlike the Meredith familiar to the novel reader, for his verse is essentially tragic, while in prose he calls himself the disciple of the comic muse. There is however a tragic note in his comedy.

Modern Love, which the poet considered his best work, consists of fifty pieces of sixteen lines so much like sonnets that Swinburne has given them the name. The story, which is partly founded on the tragedy of Meredith's first marriage, is only lightly sketched in. It tells of a tragic love. There is no villain, only a tissue of errors and misconceptions.

> "In tragic life, God wot,
> No villain need be! Passion spins the plot:
> We are betrayed by what is false within."

Had Meredith meant to tell the tale fully he would have made it into a novel; as it is, each of the fifty poems dimly discloses a phase of the story hinted, not told, or a state of mind of the principal figure. In manner of treatment the poem recalls Browning. The intellectual difficulties are like those Browning deals with, and they are as well worth solving.

From the very titles of Meredith's poems we see that he is at once the poet of nature and the poet of man. Besides *Modern Love* and *Ballads and Poems of Tragic Life*, we owe to him *Poems and Lyrics of the Joy of Earth*; besides *A Reading of Life* we owe *A Reading of Earth.* But it must not be supposed from these titles that the two are regarded by Meredith as things separate and distinct from one another: they are close akin. It is the union of the two that he praises in Shakespeare, and on that he insists in one of the finest of his nature-poems, *The Woods of Westermain.* Earth, he tells us there, is

"Spirit in her clods,
Footway to the God of Gods."

Meredith can, when he pleases, be magnificently faithful in the description of nature. *The Lark Ascending* contains the most precise and accurate description of the bird that is to be found in the whole range of English poetry; while, as poetry, the piece is worthy of comparison with Shelley's grand chain of similes. But Meredith's custom is to pass from nature to man, or from man to nature. The main stress however is laid upon humanity. From first to last Meredith is primarily the student of man, and, in the main, nature is a background to him.

From the tragic atmosphere of Meredith's poetry it is pleasant to pass on to the delightful but little-known verses of William Brighty Rands (1823—1882). We may close the chapter on poets and poetesses with the little child's address to the earth:—

"Great, wide, beautiful, wonderful World,
With the wonderful water round you curled,
And the wonderful grass upon your breast—
World, you are beautifully dressed.

The wonderful air is over me,
And the wonderful wind is shaking the tree.
It walks on the water and whirls the mills,
And talks to itself on the top of the hills.

You friendly Earth! how far do you go,
With the wheat-fields that nod, and the rivers that flow,
With cities, and gardens, and cliffs, and isles,
And people upon you for thousands of miles?

Ah, you are so great and I am so small,
I tremble to think of you, World, at all;
And yet when I said my prayers to-day,
A whisper inside me seemed to say,
'You are more than the Earth, though you are such a dot:
You can love and think, and the Earth cannot!'"

§ 1. *Some Pre-Victorian Poets.*

John Clare, 1793—1864.
Poems, descriptive of Rural Life, 1820.
Ebenezer Elliott, 1781—1849.
Corn-law Rhymes, 1831.
Thomas Hood, 1799—1845.
Lycus the Centaur, 1822.
The Plea of the Midsummer Fairies, 1827.
Hartley Coleridge, 1796—1849.
Poems, 1833.

Religious Poetry.

James Montgomery, 1771—1854.
Reginald Heber, 1783—1826.
John Keble, 1792—1866.
The Christian Year, 1827.
Lyra Innocentium, 1846.

Dramatic Poets.

James Sheridan Knowles, 1784—1862.
Virginius, 1820.
The Beggar's Daughter of Bethnal Green, 1828.
The Hunchback, 1832.
James Robinson Planché, 1796—1880.
Aubrey de Vere, 1788—1846.
Julian the Apostate, 1822.
The Duke of Mercia, 1823.
Mary Tudor, 1847.

Mary Russell Mitford, 1787—1855.
Julian, 1823.
The Foscari, 1826.
Rienzi, 1828.
Henry Taylor, 1800—1886.
Isaac Comnenus, 1827.
Philip van Artevelde, 1834.
Edwin the Fair, 1842.
The Virgin Widow, 1850.
St Clement's Eve, 1862.
Bulwer Lytton (Lord Lytton), 1803—1873.
The Duchesse de la Vallière, 1836.
The Lady of Lyons, 1838.
Richelieu, 1839.
Thomas Lovell Beddoes, 1803—1849.
The Bride's Tragedy, 1822.
Death's Jest-Book, 1850.

§ 2. *Tennyson.*

Alfred Tennyson, 1809—1892.
Poems by two Brothers (with Frederick and Charles Tennyson), 1827.
Poems, chiefly Lyrical, 1830.
Poems, 1832.
Poems, 1842.
The Princess, 1847.
In Memoriam, 1850.
Maud, 1855.
Idylls of the King, 1857—1885.
Enoch Arden, 1864.
Queen Mary, 1875.
Harold, 1876.
Becket, 1884.
Tiresias, 1885.
Locksley Hall Sixty Years After, 1886.
Demeter, 1889.
The Death of Œnone, 1892.

§ 3. *Browning.*

Robert Browning, 1812—1889.
Pauline, 1833.
Paracelsus, 1835.
Strafford, 1837.
Sordello, 1840.
Pippa Passes, 1841.
Dramatic Lyrics, 1842.
A Blot in the 'Scutcheon, 1843.
Colombe's Birthday, 1844.
Dramatic Romances and Lyrics, 1845.
Luria, 1846.
A Soul's Tragedy, 1846.
Christmas Eve and Easter Day, 1850.
Men and Women, 1855.
Dramatis Personae, 1864.
The Ring and the Book, 1868—1869.
Balaustion's Adventure, 1871.
Fifine at the Fair, 1872.
The Inn Album, 1875.
La Saisiaz, 1878.
Dramatic Idyls, 1879—1880.
Ferishtah's Fancies, 1884.
Parleyings with certain People of Importance, 1887.
Asolando, 1889.

§ 4. *Minor Singers.*

THE BALLADISTS.

Thomas Babington Macaulay, 1800—1859.
Lays of Ancient Rome, 1842.
William Edmonstoune Aytoun, 1813—1865.
Lays of the Scottish Cavaliers, 1848.
Firmilian, 1854.
Bon Gaultier Ballads (with Sir Theodore Martin), 1855.
Richard Harris Barham, 1788—1845.
The Ingoldsby Legends, 1837—1847.

WRITERS OF *Vers de Société.*

Winthrop Mackworth Praed, 1802—1839.

Richard Monckton Milnes (Lord Houghton), 1809—1885.
Memorials of a Tour in Greece, 1834.
Poems, Legendary and Historical, 1844.
Palm Leaves, 1844.

The Catholic Poets.

John Henry Newman, 1801—1890.
Lyra Apostolica (with others), 1836.
The Dream of Gerontius, 1865.
Verses on Various Occasions, 1868.
Robert Stephen Hawker, 1803—1875.
The Quest of the Sangraal, 1864.

Philosophic Poet.

Philip James Bailey, 1816—1902.
Festus, 1839.

Political Poets.

Thomas Cooper, 1805—1892.
The Purgatory of Suicides, 1845.
Capel Lofft, 1806—1873.
Ernest, or Political Regeneration, 1839.

Poet of the Celtic Revival.

James Clarence Mangan, 1803—1849.

The Poetesses.

Fanny Kemble, 1809—1893.
Francis the First, 1832.
Caroline Norton, 1808—1877.
Elizabeth Barrett Browning, 1806—1861.
An Essay on Mind, 1826.
The Seraphim, 1838.
Poems, 1844.
Sonnets from the Portuguese, 1850.
Casa Guidi Windows, 1851.
Aurora Leigh, 1857.
Poems before Congress, 1860.
Last Poems, 1862.

§ 5. *The Turn of the Century.*

Edward FitzGerald, 1809—1883.
Euphranor, 1851.
Calderon, 1853.
Rubáiyát of Omar Khayyám, 1859.

Arthur Hugh Clough, 1819—1861.
The Bothie of Tober-na-Vuolich, 1848.
Ambarvalia, 1849.
Amours de Voyage, 1858.
Dipsychus, 1862.

Matthew Arnold, 1822—1888.
The Strayed Reveller, 1849.
Empedocles on Etna, 1852.
Poems, 1853.
Merope, 1858.
Thyrsis, 1866.
New Poems, 1867.

Dante Gabriel Rossetti, 1828—1882.
The Early Italian Poets, 1861.
Poems, 1870.
Ballads and Sonnets, 1881.

Christina Rossetti, 1830—1894.
Goblin Market, 1862.
The Prince's Progress, 1866.
A Pageant, 1881.
Time Flies, 1885.

Sydney Dobell, 1824—1874.
The Roman, 1850.
Balder, 1854.
Sonnets on the War (with Alexander Smith), 1855.
England in Time of War, 1856.
The Magyar's New-Year-Eve, 1858.
The Youth of England to Garibaldi's Legion, 1860.

Alexander Smith, 1829—1867.
Poems, 1853.
City Poems, 1857.
Edwin of Deira, 1861.
Dreamthorp, 1863.
A Summer in Skye, 1865.
Alfred Hagart's Household, 1866.

Coventry Patmore, 1823—1896.
Tamerton Church Tower, 1853.
The Angel in the House, 1854—1856.
Odes, 1868.
The Unknown Eros, 1877.
Amelia, 1878.

§ 6. *The Later Pre-Raphaelites.*

William Morris, 1834—1896.
The Defence of Guenevere, 1858.
The Life and Death of Jason, 1867.
The Earthly Paradise, 1868—1870.
Sigurd the Volsung, 1876.
The House of the Wolfings, 1889.
News from Nowhere, 1891.
The Well at the World's End, 1896.
The Water of the Wondrous Isles, 1897.
The Story of the Sundering Flood, 1898.
Algernon Charles Swinburne, 1837—1909.
The Queen Mother, Rosamond, 1860.
Atalanta in Calydon, 1865.
Chastelard, 1865.
Poems and Ballads, 1866, 1878, 1889.
Songs before Sunrise, 1871.
Bothwell, 1874.
Erechtheus, 1876.
Songs of the Springtides, 1880.
Studies in Song, 1880.
Mary Stuart, 1881.
Tristram of Lyonesse, 1882.
A Century of Roundels, 1883.
Marino Faliero, 1885.
Locrine, 1887.
The Tale of Balen, 1896.
Rosamund, Queen of the Lombards, 1899.
J. B. Leicester Warren (Lord de Tabley), 1835—1895.
Philoctetes, 1866.
Orestes, 1868.
Rehearsals, 1870
Searching the Net, 1873.
Orpheus in Thrace, 1901.

§ 7. *The Celtic Poets.*

Lewis Morris, 1833—1907.
Songs of Two Worlds, 1871—1875.
The Epic of Hades, 1876—1877.
Songs Unsung, 1883.
Gycia, 1886.
Songs of Britain, 1887.
Arthur O'Shaughnessy, 1844—1881.
An Epic on Women, 1870.
Lays of France, 1872.
Music and Moonlight, 1874.
Songs of a Worker, 1881.
Aubrey de Vere, 1814—1902.
The Sisters, Inisfail, and other Poems, 1861.
The Legends of St Patrick, 1872.
Alexander the Great, 1874.
St Thomas of Canterbury, 1876.
The Foray of Queen Meave, 1882.
Robert Buchanan, 1841—1901.
Idyls and Legends of Inverburn, 1865.
London Poems, 1866.
North Coast and other Poems, 1868.
The Book of Orm, 1870
Saint Abe and his Seven Wives, 1872.
White Rose and Red, 1873.
Balder the Beautiful, 1877.
The City of Dream, 1888.
The Wandering Jew, 1893.

§ 8. *The remaining Poets.*

James Thomson, 1834—1882.
A Lady of Sorrow, 1862—1864.
Vane's Story, 1864.
Weddah and Om-el-Bonain, 1866—1867.
The City of Dreadful Night, 1874.
Philip Bourke Marston, 1850—1887.
Song Tide, 1871.
Adelaide Anne Procter, 1825—1864.
Legends and Lyrics, 1858.
A Chaplet of Verses, 1862.

Jean Ingelow, 1820—1897.
Poems, 1863, 1876, 1885.
A Story of Doom, 1867.
Augusta Webster, 1837—1894.
Dramatic Studies, 1866.
A Woman Sold, 1867.
Portraits, 1870.
The Auspicious Day, 1872.
In a Day, 1882.
The Sentence, 1887.
William Ernest Henley, 1849—1903.
A Book of Verses, 1888.
The Song of the Sword, 1892.
For England's Sake, 1900.
Hawthorn and Lavender, 1901.
Robert, Earl of Lytton (Owen Meredith), 1831—1891.
Clytemnestra, 1855.
Lucile, 1860.
Fables in Song, 1874.
Glenaveril, 1885.
After Paradise, or Legends of Exile, 1887.
Edwin Arnold, 1832—1904.
The Light of Asia, 1879.
Pearls of the Faith, 1883.
The Light of the World, 1891.
Francis Thompson, 1859—1907.
Poems, 1893.
Sister Songs, 1895.
New Poems, 1897.
George Meredith, 1828—1909.
Poems, 1851.
Modern Love, 1862.
Poems and Lyrics of the Joy of Earth, 1883.
Ballads and Poems of Tragic Life, 1887.
A Reading of Earth, 1888.
Odes in contribution to the Song of French History, 1898.
A Reading of Life, 1901.
William Brighty Rands (1823—1882).
Lilliput Levee, 1864.

CHAPTER III

NOVELS AND NOVELISTS

§ 1. *The Successors of Scott*

BEFORE dealing with the romance writers who took Sir Walter Scott as their model, it will be well to discuss one novelist who lived with Scott and for a generation after him, yet bears no trace of Scott's influence. This exception was Thomas Love Peacock (1785—1866). He was in many respects everything the author of *Waverley* was not. He was the satirist of his own generation and cared little for the past. Except for a very slight historical element in *Maid Marian* and in *The Misfortunes of Elphin*, he showed no interest in any age but his own. He neither took pleasure in the delineation of the normal human character, nor could find any charm in that commonplace life which supplied Scott with his richest materials.

There is little to tell about Peacock's personal history. His knowledge was acquired without the help of school or university, but it was sufficient, at least in classics, to satisfy the tolerably exacting judgment of Macaulay, who records that he and Peacock tested each other's knowledge in Greek and found they were both "strong enough in these matters for gentlemen."

In poetry, which was the first form of literature that he tried, he was at his best in the lyric or ballad. Scattered through his stories we find exquisite snatches of songs grave and gay. His comic verse is excellent. But the comic and satirical genius finds its best expression in prose, and the change from verse to the prose tale was a happy one for Peacock. His stories and plots however count for little; they are mere threads on which to hang the satire. In *Melincourt* we find him laughing at the abolition of slavery and at the Lake Poets. In *Nightmare Abbey* he holds up to ridicule Byron as Mr Cypress, Coleridge as Mr Flosky and Southey as Mr Sackbut. Even Shelley, as Mr Scythrop, does not escape. Shelley was the only writer of his time whom Peacock really liked and admired; and though his affection did not prevent him from caricaturing Shelley, it did restrain him from going far enough to break the friendship. Shelley enjoyed the laugh as much as the readers, and continued to be the author's friend until his death. *The Misfortunes of Elphin*, *Crotchet Castle* and *Gryll Grange* show the influence of prosperity. Their author looks with more lenient eyes on the follies of the world, and laughs more joyously at the absurdities of the Steam Intellect Society and the March of Mind. But his works will never be popular reading. They have beauty of style and sparkling wit, they show knowledge and technical skill; but his characters lack reality, and, though we laugh, we do not feel that the creatures we are laughing at are real men and women.

Peacock is, as it were, on a side track; the direct line of development in fiction lay through Scott, and the vein which was most diligently worked in the years immediately after him was that of the historical romance. Scott was not indeed the first to write historical novels, but nevertheless he may be considered the father of this form of fiction in England, France and Germany. The great popularity of the Waverley novels stimulated story-tellers to try what treasures their wits could discover in the records of the past. But they read in order that they might write, while Scott wrote from the fulness of knowledge already acquired. The consequence is that their books smell of musty records and of midnight oil.

William Harrison Ainsworth (1805—1882) was one of the story-tellers who worked heavily and laboriously on the lines of Scott. His *Tower of London*, *Old St Paul's* and *Windsor Castle* are monuments of industry; but they are tiresome reading, and even at times repulsive, because of the gruesome details of cruel acts and horrible deaths which have been collected. Yet the school-masters of his time presented his books as prizes to the schoolboys.

Scott set the fashion in other things as well as in historical fiction. No writer is more deeply imbued with the spirit of nationality. His stories of Scottish life conferred on Scotland, as it has been phrased, a citizenship of letters. Here too he had followers. Scott's own son-in-law, Lockhart, worked in this field, though there is little resemblance between his *Adam Blair* and anything of Scott's. Neither have the sentimental tales of John Wilson, better known by his pseudonym Christopher North, much of Scott's spirit. They were nevertheless suggested by the Waverley series. So too were the stories of John Galt (1779—1839), which have far more of the genius of the master. Galt, in fact, attempted to do for the estate of Kittlestonheugh what Scott did for Scotland. He wrote the *Annals of the Parish* with admirable insight and complete fidelity; and though that is the title of only one of his stories, it indicates the spirit and method of all. What he could not do was to depict that larger world into which Scott takes us, or to rise, in his narrower world, to the heights of tragedy which Scott reaches in the story of the Mucklebackits.

In Ireland also there was a group of young writers who set themselves the task of doing for their country what the author of *Waverley* had done for Scotland. Unfortunately they lacked not only the genius but the education which was needful for the historical part at least of the work. This deficiency is sadly apparent in William Carleton (1794—1869), the most highly gifted of these Irishmen. It did not prevent him from writing excellent stories of the life with which he was familiar—stories incomparably more faithful and better grounded than the caricatures of the far more famous Lever. Unfortunately Carleton is better known east of St George's Channel by the comparatively weak and poor tale of *Willy Reilly*. The work by which he best deserves to be known is his extraordinarily vivid and interesting *Autobiography*. Some of Carleton's statements in that book should perhaps be taken with caution. Many would be disposed to doubt whether he is accurate when he asserts that in his first day at school he learnt his alphabet, and had advanced in spelling as far as b, a, g, bag. There is unfortunately less reason to doubt his more important statement that he remembered the time when there was "no law *against* an Orangeman, and no law *for* a Papist." But whatever deductions may be made, it is safe to assert that this *Autobiography* is one of the most valuable documents in existence for the study of Irish life in the nineteenth century. For this and for his *Traits and Stories of the Irish Peasantry* Carleton deserves exceedingly well of his country. Several more of Carleton's stories are well worth reading, but the spirit of all his work is present in the *Traits and Stories*.

Among his Irish contemporaries Carleton rightly thought that those who were most worthy to stand beside himself were John Banim and Gerald Griffin. Both were respectable writers, but neither of them left work which has any title to be called great. They died comparatively young, and probably the writings they left do not adequately express their gifts.

An Irishman of a different class was William Maginn (1793—1842). His actual writings are less valuable than those of the men above named, but he contrived to stamp his mark more deeply upon the literature of his time. Under the pseudonym of O'Doherty he contributed to *Blackwood's Magazine* and became one of the most prominent of the brilliant band who were associated with it. There seem to have been few periodicals of the time with which he had not something to do. But his great achievement was the establishment, with the help of his friend Hugh Fraser, of *Fraser's Magazine*, to which he attracted a body of writers more brilliant than even that of *Blackwood*. By this ceaseless journalism Maginn wrote himself out, without ever having done the work he was born to do. His great talent and his unquestionable scholarship are represented only by a miscellaneous collection from which the spirit has almost wholly evaporated. He will live longer as the Captain Shandon of Thackeray than for anything he himself has left. For a time however, partly by his own writings and partly by the writings of the friends whom he gathered round him, Maginn gave a markedly Irish flavour to *Fraser's Magazine*. Among those friends were Crofton Croker, who collected and reduced to form the interesting *Fairy Legends and Traditions of the South of Ireland*, and Francis Mahony, who is better known by his pen-name of Father Prout, author of the famous *Reliques*. Few probably would have the patience now to read the *Reliques* through; their wit is stale; and yet they saved *Fraser's Magazine* from the ruin with which the immortal *Sartor Resartus* of Carlyle had threatened it.

It is unfortunate that English impressions of Ireland have been drawn mainly, not from Carleton, but from two caricaturists, Samuel Lover (1797—1868) and Charles Lever (1806—1872). There are several points of resemblance between them. Both, in particular, were excellent writers of humorous songs: the former's *Widow Machree* and the latter's *Widow Malone* are admirable as pieces of fun in verse. But except in this point Lever was decidedly the greater man of the two. It is strange that this typical Irishman, as he is supposed to be, was Irish by little more than birth. His father migrated from Manchester, and his mother too traced her origin to an English family. By far the best known of Lever's tales are his earliest, *Harry Lorrequer* and *Charles O'Malley*, and the latter is probably that which best deserves to be known. It is true that in later days Lever's methods became somewhat less crude than they are in that lively story, and he himself preferred some of the works of his maturer years; but probably more was lost in verve than was gained in finish. Lever is a writer who must not be taken too seriously. His most authentically Irish characteristic is his cheerful carelessness. To use his own words, he wrote as he lived, from hand to mouth. There was no time to give care and labour to the work, even if he had possessed the critical power necessary to polish it. The printer's devil was always waiting on the doorstep, or the dun for his money in the passage.

Some of Lever's stories are superficially historical, but the history is a very thin veneer. The spirit in which he treated it is shown in the bargain he made with a certain officer of the British army, who by a legal deed sold to Lever for four napoleons the right to make what use the novelist pleased of his adventures. This personage figures in Lever's pages as Major Monsoon. But slight as the historical element is, its presence gives Lever a place among the novelists who were inspired by the gigantic struggle with Napoleon. Among others stirred by the incidents of these wars may be mentioned William Hamilton Maxwell and George Robert Gleig, whose autobiographic tale, *The Subaltern*, won the admiration of Wellington, and ultimately led to Gleig's becoming the biographer of the great duke. James Grant wrote a good deal later. His *Romance of War* is considered by many to be the best of all the stories suggested by the Peninsular War.

The triumphs of Nelson as well as the glories of Wellington had their story-tellers, and Frederick Marryat (1792—1848) has done for the sailor what Lever tried to do for the soldier. By profession a seaman, he enjoyed the interesting experience of working for three years under the great commander Cochrane, afterwards Lord Dundonald, whom we meet as Captain Savage in the novel *Peter Simple*. On the famous ship Impérieuse Marryat saw fifty engagements and was wounded three times. When he took to writing he had gathered together an immense collection of adventures and had met many unusual characters. As they all belonged to an epoch of seafaring life which has passed away with the invention of steamships and the development of machinery, his novels will always be of interest as the best pictures of the great age of English sea power. The most readable of them, in addition to that already named, are *Jacob Faithful* and *Midshipman Easy*. They are written in a style careless indeed and boisterous, but for that very reason well fitted to the subject, and as pictures of a bygone form of life they deserve a permanent place in literature.

Another important writer of fiction, who won a higher place in his lifetime than posterity has seen fit to accord him, was Lord Lytton, who was first known as Edward Bulwer (1803—1873). He started writing in his teens, and at Cambridge carried off the Chancellor's medal. After achieving this distinction he cut himself off from his friends and joined a roving band of gypsies, one of whose daughters he wedded after the manner of these wandering tribes. In 1827 he made a regular marriage with a lady of his own race, but the union brought him no happiness. Mrs Bulwer, brilliant, beautiful and miserable, took the public into her confidence in order to make money, and also to revenge herself for the wrongs, real and imaginary, inflicted upon her by her husband. As Bulwer's mother was alienated from her son by the marriage, he became dependent on the earnings his pen could bring him. He spent money so lavishly that he was forced to work beyond his strength; and this hurried work was unworthy of his powers. Yet in spite of this pressure, and though he was handicapped by deafness and an impediment in his speech, Lytton played a part in politics also and won his way to cabinet rank. It is astonishing to read that men listening to his oratory felt he was almost the greatest of speakers. So too in the literary world his books were spoken of as works of the highest genius. Charles Reade, adapting Byron's saying about Sheridan, declared that Lytton had "written the best play, the best comedy and the best novel of the age." Thackeray however was not dazzled by the glamour, and James Thomson, the author of *The City of Dreadful Night*, spoke scornfully of Lytton's "pinchbeck poetry, pinchbeck philosophy, pinchbeck learning, pinchbeck sentiment." Perhaps his failure to do really great work was the result of his versatility. He tried oratory, poetry, dramas, novels of manners, historical romances, mystical tales, ghost stories, and all the manifold and weird forms of literature which come from the brain of a man who believes in the supernatural. Even until his death his name stirred the imagination and excited interest. It seemed right to bury him in Westminster Abbey, but few now think that his proper resting place is there.

Lytton's early novels, *Falkland*, *Paul Clifford* and *Eugene Aram* are not healthy reading; they are morbid studies of crime. *The Last Days of Pompeii*, *Rienzi* and the romances founded on English history are imitations of Scott. Then there is a group of stories, *The Caxtons*, *My Novel* and *What will he do with It?* which are his contribution to the fashion of writing novels of domestic life. But Lytton could not wholly rid himself of affectation, a vice peculiarly objectionable in work of this sort. Perhaps only his tales of the supernatural were absolutely sincere. There was no other subject which interested him more deeply, or came nearer to being a religion to him. Of this class the best known is *Zanoni*, the history of a man who at the call of love voluntarily gives up immortality, the secret of which he has won.

In this phase of his mind Lytton stands far apart from his fellow novelist Benjamin Disraeli (1804—1881), afterwards Earl of Beaconsfield, who took no pleasure in any magic that was not of his own world. Yet Disraeli was not unlike Lytton in the brilliant versatility of his genius. Their lives too ran on somewhat parallel lines. Both were politicians, both changed sides, and both left a curious mixture of admiration and distrust in the minds of their contemporaries.

Disraeli was one of the most picturesque figures of the early thirties. A contemporary says, "His evening coat was of black velvet lined with satin, purple trousers with a gold band running down the outside seam, a scarlet waistcoat, long lace ruffles falling down to the tips of his fingers, white gloves with several brilliant rings outside them, and long black ringlets rippling down upon his shoulders." The figure is singularly un-English; and this was in part the reason of the deep dislike with which Disraeli was long regarded. *Punch* satirised him with a bitterness unusual in those genial pages. Lockhart called him a "Jew scamp," and other contemptuous terms, such as "swab" and "traitor," were flung at him. In truth he was a child of the East, full of visions of the glory of his race and of his own destiny, all of which he took seriously. Many of his visions he went far towards realising. He forced the English country gentry to accept as their leader an alien whom they distrusted, and he also, alien as he was, crowned Victoria Empress of India and secured for England a controlling interest in the Suez Canal.

Politics, not literature, was Disraeli's great interest, and in this respect he is the opposite of Lytton. In *Vivian Grey*, a novel of society like Bulwer's *Pelham*, we have a brilliant picture of a young adventurer forcefully making his way by his own wits. In that light the world regarded Disraeli himself. But *Vivian Grey* fails, and Disraeli did not mean to fail. There is however more romance than business in the story. It is not until we read the three famous books which came out in the forties, *Coningsby*, *Sybil* and *Tancred*, that we understand the strength as well as the weakness of their author. In these books he enlarges upon the schemes of reform which had begun to occupy him when he entered parliament in 1837 and gradually became more prominent in his mind as he advanced in position and power, until on his election in 1848 to be leader of the opposition he found himself strong enough to try to make them realities. The doctrine he sought to inculcate was that the comfort and wellbeing of the people ought to be the first aim of governments. Schemes for social legislation were rare in his day, and Disraeli by his insistence upon their importance showed himself a far-seeing statesman and in some cases a prophet.

For many years the pressure of politics prevented Disraeli from writing. His last books came out towards the end of his life. His interests had now become entirely political, his life lay behind him, he had lost the eager hopes and expectations which gave his earlier works their prophetic fervour and the characters their vivid though somewhat glaring colour. *Lothair* and *Endymion* are dull reading.

§ 2. *Dickens*

Dickens and Thackeray are the real successors of Scott, for, though they did not imitate him, it was they who carried on and modified the tradition of the English novel. Their work is more realistic than Scott's. Though both of them wrote historical novels, this particular type of romance had at first little attraction for them, and the middle ages, the favourite field of historical story-tellers, had none at all. They preferred to turn their searchlights upon their own time or on the very recent past. Dickens found in the streets of London practically all the materials he required for his stories of his own day; Thackeray drew from a wider area in space and in time, but his main study was the society of his own generation in the upper and middle classes.

Charles Dickens (1812—1870) was the son of a clerk in the Navy pay-office, and much of the history of his miserable childhood has been given to us in his account of David Copperfield. Dickens himself worked in the blacking warehouse. In the easy-going, careless Mr Micawber we have a portrait of John Dickens the father; and the mysterious "deeds" which, in this novel, lead up to imprisonment in the Marshalsea, were really executed by him. To the end of his life Dickens remembered with bitterness the miseries and degradations of those years. The education he received at school was trifling, and at fifteen he entered a lawyer's office, where he remained a year and a half. He gave up his legal work in order to be a reporter on the staff of *The True Sun*, in which capacity he became, in his own words, "the best and most rapid reporter ever known." But he had higher ambitions. He judged himself, and truly, to be fit for the stage, and began to train himself to be an actor. Luckily for posterity, he was diverted from his purpose. It was about this time that he started writing down his own thoughts as well as reporting those of others. His first production, known to us now as *Mr Minns and his Cousin*, one of the *Sketches by Boz*, was printed in *The Monthly Magazine* in 1833. The young novelist has described his nervous hopes and fears when he dropped his little story into the letter box of the magazine. Three years later the *Sketches by Boz*, sketches so hopefully begun, had become known, and Dickens was invited to write *The Pickwick Papers*, which made him at once the most popular novelist of his age, and still constitutes his best title to fame. The success of this work was swift and brilliant. Only four hundred copies of the first number were ordered. Forty thousand were ordered of the fifteenth.

Henceforth Dickens was a writer by profession, and there is little more to record of personal history beyond his marriage, which became unhappy, the attainment of his highest boyish ambition in the purchase of the house known as Gad's Hill Place, the dates of his books, two visits to America, and various peregrinations through England as an entertainer reading aloud from his books. It was in the forties that Dickens conceived the plan of giving these readings; but his best friends dissuaded him from making this public display of himself. However, in 1858 he insisted on starting, and Carlyle, who witnessed one of his exhibitions, saw in Dickens reading his own novel "a whole tragic, comic, heroic, *theatre* visible, performing under one *hat*"; and performing extraordinarily well, for he added that Dickens "acts better than any Macready in the world." Forster, the friend and adviser and ultimately the biographer of Dickens, felt that these displays were in bad taste. But Dickens persisted, partly from love of gain, for he netted about £45,000, and partly because he himself got pleasure from the readings.

As a rule the plots of Dickens's novels are not successful, though the unfinished *Mystery of Edwin Drood* shows that, when he chose to devote himself to the task of making one, he could surpass his contemporaries in the art of construction, as well as in the delineation of character. But he felt himself restrained and handicapped by the uncongenial necessity; and for this reason he did his best work in such books as *The Pickwick Papers*, where he was free to go whither his fancy led.

By his education in the university of the streets Dickens had unconsciously given himself the best preparation for such novels as *Oliver Twist*, *David Copperfield* and *Nicholas Nickleby*. But at the same time he had narrowed his world to the inhabitants of those streets. Some of his critics say that he has never been able to describe a gentleman. Though the figure of Sydney Carton is enough to show that this judgment is too sweeping, it is certainly true to say that Dickens was never so much at home as when he was dealing with the Londoner of the lower ranks. His books teem with such people, sufficient in number, it has been said, to send a member to parliament. They are a curious collection, following strange and unfamiliar trades—there is the man who lives by recovering bodies from the Thames, the articulator of skeletons, the dustman, the midwife, the chimney-sweeper, the housebreaker. Dickens knew them all, better than most of us know our next-door neighbour. In the country he was out of his element. If by any chance his characters move thither they carry the town with them. Dickens has had many imitators. The shelves of our bookshops are full of stories of mean streets. But though these may have more of the truth of a photograph than the stories of Dickens, yet we feel that there is a deeper truth which he has and they have not. To him the dwellers in the city slums have joys as well as sorrows and privations, and they are as profoundly human as their superiors in social position. What strikes us above all in his delineations of slum-land is their rich fun and humour.

It was by these qualities mainly that he won success in *Pickwick.* But when he wrote *The Old Curiosity Shop* and *Dombey and Son* it was what they called pathos and we are tempted to call sentimentality that the critics and general readers applauded most. Macaulay wept over Florence Dombey, Jeffrey spoke of "the divine Nelly," and Thackeray felt he had not "an atom of a chance" against such "stupendous writing" as the death of little Paul. George Eliot and Ruskin however thought otherwise. The wind has now veered to their quarter, and most people would agree with Mr W. D. Howells when he pronounces the pathetic scenes in *The Old Curiosity Shop* "preposterously overdone." We have become restless under the preachings of Pecksniff and impatient of the monotonous humility of Uriah Heep; but we still laugh with Sam Weller and laugh at Mrs Gamp, and we still enjoy the sportsmanship of Mr Winkle. It may therefore be safely said that it is by reason of his humorous characters that Dickens will keep his place in English hearts.

§ 3. *Thackeray*

William Makepeace Thackeray (1811—1863) was born in Calcutta and came home to England for his education. Napoleon was then a prisoner on the island of St Helena, and the boy had a glimpse of the deposed Emperor. He did not take kindly to his English school, the Charterhouse; in his earlier writings it figures as the Swishtail Academy; but time mellowed his memory, and in *The Newcomes* we read of it under the name of the Grey Friars. From the Charterhouse Thackeray went to Cambridge, where he was slightly Tennyson's junior. After leaving college he visited Germany, where he made the acquaintance of Goethe. In 1831 he was back in England and preparing for the bar; but he seems to have shown no more zeal in getting ready for that profession than his hero Pendennis did. His successor in chambers found his desk crammed with sketches and caricatures. Thackeray had unfortunately inherited a small fortune from his father, and so he did not feel the healthy compulsion of necessity to work. He spent much time lying awake at nights considering how he would use his money. Whatever he may have resolved to do with it, he lost all in newspaper speculation a few years after he had obtained control of it. He married in 1836, and was very happy, living mainly in Paris, until the mental breakdown of his wife made his home desolate and left him with the care of two practically motherless little girls. In the *Ballad of Bouillabaisse* there are allusions to this terrible time.

Thackeray was both artist and man of letters. At the beginning of his life he even leaned to the pencil rather than to the pen. But he could not draw, and it is fortunate for the world that in the end literature rather than art became his calling. He continued to illustrate his own books, and, faulty though his drawings are, as aids to the text his illustrations are admirable. It is his pencil which strips off the gorgeous ermine mantle of the royal Ludovicus Rex, and puts beside it the poor little shivering "forked radish" Ludovicus.

Thackeray's early writings were mainly produced for periodicals—*Fraser's Magazine, The New Monthly Magazine, The Times.* From 1842 to 1854 he was a regular contributor to *Punch*, for which he only ceased to write because he did not sympathise with its attitude towards Napoleon III. *The Book of Snobs*, one of the most characteristic of Thackeray's works, is composed of articles which originally appeared in *Punch. The Yellowplush Papers, The Great Hoggarty Diamond* and *Barry Lyndon* came out in *Fraser's Magazine.* All these, as well as the *Paris* and *Irish Sketch Books* and the *Notes of a Journey from Cornhill to Grand Cairo,* belong to the first period of Thackeray's work, which may be taken to end in 1846. *Vanity Fair,* which appeared in 1847—1848, was the first work of his second and greater period. In the earlier list *Barry Lyndon,* the autobiography of a scoundrel, gave proof of very great intellectual force, but it can never take rank with his highest efforts, *Vanity Fair, Esmond, Pendennis* and *The Newcomes.* These were all, except *Esmond,* written to the call of the printer waiting for copy, and with this one exception they are faulty in construction. From the fact that *Esmond* is singularly well constructed we may infer that, had Thackeray been sufficiently provident and strenuous to write his story beforehand, he would have ranked among the masters of the art of construction.

Esmond is a historical novel, the scene of which is laid in the time of Queen Anne. *The Virginians* also is historical; as is likewise the fragment *Denis Duval,* which Thackeray did not live to finish. We know too that he thought and talked in his family about another historical subject which he never even began to treat. It seems therefore that *Esmond* was no mere chance excursion into the field of history. It indicates the growth in his mind of the romantic element and a partial abandonment of the more realistic themes with which he started. Nevertheless, because of the predominant character of what he wrote during his great period, Thackeray must remain for us essentially a realist—meaning here by that word a man who was determined to depict life as it actually was and as he knew it. *Pendennis* and *The Newcomes* are both pictures of the modern world with its virtues unheightened and its vices unconcealed—or at least concealed no more than was made necessary by a sense of decency, as some would say, or of prudery, as others would call it. But we must be on our guard against supposing that every work necessarily depicts the whole world. In a most illuminating sentence regarding *Vanity Fair* Thackeray tells us that he intended "to make a set of people living without God in the world (only that is a cant phrase), greedy, pompous men, perfectly satisfied for the most part, and at ease about their superior virtue." In this book his Crawleys, Sedleys, and Lord Steyne are all he meant them to be. We can see then that to the charge that he gives a one-sided view Thackeray would reply that he never meant to give anything else. But the reply is not convincing. The impression produced is in point of fact wrong, and the method is not the method of Shakespeare, who balances evil with a weight of good which bears a fair proportion to it. It is true that Thackeray makes us recognise evil and loathe it. He also leads us on until we see the evildoer enter into a hell of his own creation and shut behind him by his own actions the door of escape. Beatrix Esmond spent her life breaking hearts, and we see her ending it in unrespected old age. Thackeray is always teaching us that we cannot escape the law of the harvest. We must reap in autumn what we sow in spring. We resent this preaching, and yet again we call him cynic. The judgment of Charlotte Brontë is a worthy answer to that charge, if the creator of such noble characters as Colonel Esmond and Colonel Newcome needs any defence. "Whenever," she says, "Thackeray writes, Mephistopheles stands on his right hand and Raphael on his left; the great doubter and sneerer usually guides the pen, the angel, noble and gentle, interlines letters of light here and there." Still, as there is no smoke without fire, so the charge of cynicism against Thackeray has a certain truth behind it, as also has the criticism that he produced novels without heroes, that his characters are, with few exceptions, morally commonplace, or worse. To this charge he answers that the really great are very rare. The answer is true; but it is also true that they are of first-rate importance, and to ignore them is a grave mistake.

Besides writing books Thackeray lectured both in England and in America. The lectures were the most profitable of all his literary enterprises, the two sets, *The English Humourists of the Eighteenth Century* and *The Four Georges*, bringing him in a total of £9500. The *Humourists*, like *Esmond*, illustrates his profound knowledge of the eighteenth century, as well as his fine literary taste. No one else has ever made himself live in that period as Thackeray did. No one else has so marvellously caught its true style as he does in *Esmond.*

Thackeray died very suddenly on Christmas eve at the age of fifty-two. He left unfinished *Denis Duval*, of which Dickens wrote: "In respect of earnest feeling, far-seeing purpose, character, incident, and a certain loving picturesqueness blending the whole, I believe it to be much the best of all his works." He left no successor or disciple, unless it was George du Maurier (1834—1896) whose *Trilby* has more of Thackeray's spirit than any other book in English.

§ 4. *Women Novelists*

Before considering individually the women novelists of the Victorian period it will be interesting to see how they appeared to the great French statesman and historian Guizot, and how much superior he found their work to that of his own countrywomen. "I am a great novel reader," he says, "but I seldom read German or French novels. The characters are too artificial. There are too many forced situations, and the morality is generally detestable. My delight is to read English novels, particularly those written by women. *C'est toute une école de morale.* Miss Austen, Miss Ferrier, Charlotte Brontë, George Eliot, Mrs Gaskell, and many others almost as remarkable, form a school which in the excellence, the profusion, and the contemporaneousness of its productions, resembles the crowd of dramatic poets of the great Athenian age." This remarkable tribute of praise is justified by an examination of the work women have accomplished in this branch of literature. In no other sphere do they rise to the first rank. There has never been a female Shakespeare; but the famous French critic Scherer finds George Eliot the first of English novelists, and he is not alone in this judgment.

The three Brontë sisters have a niche in literature all to themselves. They were Charlotte Brontë (1816—1855), Emily Brontë (1818—1848) and Anne Brontë (1820—1849). Their father was the Rev. Patrick Brontë, an Irish Protestant of County Down and an Orangeman. He was given to writing occasional verse. In 1820 he was offered the desolate vicarage of Haworth in the lonely Yorkshire moors, and moved thither with his six children, five girls and one boy, who was then the idol of the home, but who lived to be its greatest sorrow. The father led a secluded studious life in the bleak parsonage, where the children were wholly given up to drawing, dreaming, reading books meant for their seniors, and wandering alone over the wild moors. Ultimately the girls were sent to a school at Cowan Bridge. Two of them died there, and the younger sisters were taken away in 1825. The genius of Charlotte has given us a picture of the miseries of "Lowood" School: the tragic fate of her sister Maria is told in *Jane Eyre* in the heartrending account of the consumptive girl Helen Burns, with her racking cough, dying in the cold fireless dormitory. It was during these school days that Charlotte heard the story of the man with the mad wife, who felt himself morally free to leave her and marry again; and this story suggested to her the idea of Rochester in the same novel. The history of the second period of the school life of the Brontë girls has been embodied in *Shirley*, and their third and last educational experience in Brussels furnished material for the two novels *Villette* and *The Professor*.

Charlotte Brontë only wrote these four novels. *The Professor*, though it was not published till after her death, is an earlier and cruder performance than the others. When she offered it for publication the publishers thought it wanting in excitement and interest, and they told her so. With characteristic good sense the authoress recognised her mistake and set about correcting it. In *Jane Eyre* the heroine is a governess, plain and homely, but fascinating; the hero is an improbable and unpleasant person who pursues his wooing in Byronic fashion; and the scene is laid in a terrible house where the upper story is used as an asylum for the mad wife. The incidents are a dinner party, a country walk and a fire. Yet out of these unromantic materials Charlotte Brontë made a story which enthralled men like Lockhart, G. H. Lewes and Thackeray. Thus she became the "daughter of debate," discussed everywhere, and fêted and lionised when she visited London at the suggestion of her publishers. The best part of her book relates to her school experiences. In all the Brontë writings there is scarcely anything good which cannot be traced back to incidents in their own lives. For this reason it is doubtful whether, had they lived longer, they would have been able to add much of value to their writings.

The early plan the sisters cherished of holding a school in Haworth Vicarage being made impossible by the dissipated habits of their brother, after the success of *Jane Eyre* they gave themselves up to literary work at home. Their lives were hard, cheerless and full of suffering. There was little cause for laughter in their home, and in their books the want of mirth is a marked defect. Emily especially was full of gloom and harsh reserve. The story told in *Shirley* of the mad dog happened to her. When the animal bit her she applied cautery with her own hand, telling no one until after the danger was over.

Charlotte, writing of her in the biographical sketch, says that she was "stronger than a man, simpler than a child, her nature stood alone." Arnold wrote that her soul—

> "Knew no fellow for might,
> Passion, vehemence, grief,
> Daring, since Byron died."

Of *Wuthering Heights* Dante Rossetti said that "the action is laid in hell, only it seems places and people have English names there." Her verse includes a few pieces of rare excellence. Of the three sisters Emily alone possessed the gift of poetry. What this great gloomy genius might have become had she lived her full span, no one can say; but she died at thirty, "torn," her sister says, "conscious, panting, reluctant, though resolute, out of a happy life." Anne was a contrast. She died leaving as her farewell to the world some verses whose meek submissiveness makes them very touching. She was by far the weakest of the sisters, and but for Charlotte and Emily her name would not be remembered.

Charlotte was now left alone. Six years after Emily's death she married her father's curate Mr Nicholls, who appears in *Shirley* as Mr McCarthy. It is said that he was not the hero of her dreams; yet on her deathbed a year later, as her life was ebbing out "she caught the sound of some murmured words of prayer that God would spare her. 'Oh,' she whispered forth, 'I am not going to die, am I? He will not separate us, we have been so happy.'" This description of her last moments is given in the beautiful biography written by her friend and fellow craftswoman Mrs Gaskell.

We think of Mrs Gaskell primarily as a novelist, but by virtue of *The Life of Charlotte Brontë* she is also one of the very small group of writers who have enriched literature with biographies of permanent worth. Elizabeth Cleghorn

Gaskell (1810—1865) was the daughter of William Stevenson, at one time a Unitarian minister. She was born at Knutsford, in Cheshire, the old-world village which she has immortalised as Cranford. It lies almost within sound of the busy hum of the manufacturing towns of Lancashire, but was then asleep itself with the stillness of perpetual Sunday. Miss Stevenson married a Unitarian minister living in Manchester, and in that city she found materials for the novels which give us pictures of the struggle between capital and labour about the middle of last century. In *Mary Barton* Mrs Gaskell tried to rouse sympathy on behalf of the workers and to show the evils which had grown up with the factory system. She saw that the employers of labour too often felt no responsibility for their workmen, and lived in luxury themselves, while their hands were herded together like brutes. The picture of the employer Carson in this book aroused much angry feeling among the masters; and perhaps in *North and South* she was trying to balance matters when she introduced the character of Thornton, who, though not faultless, has more sympathy with his work-folk than the brutal Carson. She recognised that the evils of the factory system were not the outcome of wickedness on the side either of the employers or the employed, but were due to the absence of kindly human relations between them. This truth she set herself to preach in her later Lancashire stories.

But Mrs Gaskell's work of highest merit is *Cranford*. Had she written a few more books like it, she must have ranked among the best of English novelists. Her forty odd stories have much that we value. Grace, goodness and kindliness of heart are never absent from them, and for these qualities and her gentle mirth Mrs Gaskell ranks with Charles Lamb and Goldsmith among the authors we not only admire but love.

Mrs Gaskell's great contemporary Mary Ann Evans, who is better known to us as George Eliot (1819—1880), was born in Warwickshire just nine years after her. The old Elizabethan houses, thatched cottages, green lanes and rich parks of that county are to her work what the quiet landscapes of Cheshire, or the barren rugged moorlands of Yorkshire were to her sister novelists. Her father was a land agent and farmer near Coventry, her mother died when she was seventeen, and she had then to take up the duties of mistress of her father's house. She took great pride in her butter and cheese making and in the general excellence of her household management, and held to the end of her life a high opinion of the life of practical usefulness for women. "Did you not then find enough to interest you in your family?" was the question she addressed to a mother who had published a novel. Apparently George Eliot thought that had she been given the privilege of being the mother of children she would not have written books.

In early life Miss Evans found time to study French, German, Italian and the classics. To music she was devoted. She was also deeply religious. But after her removal with her father to the nearer neighbourhood of Coventry she came under influences which greatly strengthened certain doubts she had begun to feel, and caused her to change her views and to refuse to go to church. At a later date she regretted her refusal because of the pain it gave her father; but her opinions never moved back to the current views of church-goers. She was profoundly interested in the subject and her earliest writings were upon religious topics. She translated Strauss's *Life of Jesus* and Feuerbach's *Essence of Christianity*. This proof of scholarship procured for her the post of assistant editor of *The Westminster Review*, to which her most notable contribution is her paper on *Worldliness and Other-Worldliness*.

It was not until her friend G. H. Lewes, who ultimately became her husband, suggested fiction to her that she found her true calling. *Amos Barton*, the first of the *Scenes of Clerical Life*, was introduced by Lewes to the Blackwoods as the work of a sensitive and diffident friend; and it was during the correspondence with the publishers that the name of George Eliot was adopted. The sensitiveness and diffidence were real, and it is said that she handled her latest works with the same trembling fingers and nervous bearing as when she was still an unknown writer. The clerical scenes made the new writer famous; while the great novels *Adam Bede, The Mill on the Floss*, and *Silas Marner* raised her to a position among the foremost living writers.

As George Eliot painted her landscapes from the scenes she knew, so she drew her characters from the people among whom she lived. Her father, mother, brother, sister, her aunt and herself, all appear in those early novels. When this rich vein of reminiscences and of old memories threatened to become exhausted she felt she must search for new material. She therefore turned to Italy, to politics and history, and to the problems of race for her subjects. So it came about that in *Romola* we learn of the great religious conflict of the fifteenth century in Florence; in *Felix Holt* we are back in England watching the struggle between the conservative upper class and the radical reformer Felix; in *Daniel Deronda* we are taken among the Hebrews and are directed to the problems of heredity and to the social difficulties of the English Jew. There is effort and strain in these books, they represent much knowledge, and cost their creator considerable pain to produce. They are admirable of their kind, but all inferior to the more spontaneous early novels. *Middlemarch* takes its place among her great works, because in it she writes again of English country life, of the things she has always known, the things that are part of herself.

Touches of delightful humour are not absent from the books in which she went outside her own experiences, but they are rare; and in these books we should not, as we do in *Adam Bede*, recognise humour as one of her principal gifts. In that novel and in *The Mill on the Floss* her characters are not, it is true, conscious mirth-makers, like Falstaff, but they are unconsciously amusing. George Eliot had actually heard the delightful conversations of Mrs Poyser and her sisters upon cooking recipes, bed-covers and other treasured family heirlooms and belongings. It is in such simple homely scenes that she reveals her sense of humour.

Sympathy is another of the characteristics of George Eliot, and it comes out very prominently in her treatment of religion and of clergymen. In her attitude towards ministers of religion she contrasts strikingly with Charlotte Brontë, who seldom introduces a clerical character into her pages without a sneer at him. Perhaps the absence of any creed in the mind of George Eliot and the struggles she had made to retain one gave her a fuller comprehension of the mental difficulties of the clerical life, just as her own very debatable action in marriage made her unusually sensitive to the sacredness of the bond and the great beauty and high possibilities of wedded life. In her books George Eliot makes marriage the source of nearly all tragedy, as well as of the deepest happiness in life. It is the influence which either makes or mars a character.

George Eliot's mind had a very argumentative bias. She was driven by her intellect to question everything. "I admit discussion," she says, "upon every matter except dinners and debts. I hold that the first must be eaten and the second must be paid. These are my only prejudices." This philosophic attitude is judged a virtue by the critics who think her most learned and philosophical novels the best. That was the view of some contemporaries, but of very few at the present day. To Swinburne these novels showed how irretrievably and intolerably wrong it was possible for even the highest intellect, as distinguished from genius, to go.

George Eliot died in December 1880, having in the early part of the same year married her second husband Mr J. W. Cross, who has written her biography.

Among the other female writers of fiction, whose name is legion, there is none to rival George Eliot in power and range of thought, or Charlotte Brontë in passion, nor is there any to whom literature is indebted for such a gem as *Cranford.* Probably not a single novel they have written will be read half a century hence except by a few students. There are however two or three who demand notice because of their temporary fame, and one, Mrs Oliphant, for powers which, if she had not been obliged to write in order to live, might have gained for her a permanent place in literature.

Margaret Oliphant (1828—1897) began her work with the novel of *Margaret Maitland,* about which the critic Jeffrey wrote that nothing so true and touching had appeared as a picture of Scottish life since Galt's *Annals of the Parish.* Mrs Oliphant's best stories treat of Scotland and Scotch people. Outside that sphere perhaps her greatest successes were the series known as *The Chronicles of Carlingford,* where she was bold enough to venture upon ground not unlike that which George Eliot had made her own. Mrs Oliphant was a very rapid and easy writer, and amidst her many domestic cares in the rearing and educating of a family she managed to produce good biographies and other books less good, besides the innumerable stories which poured from her pen. Yet her family said they never knew when she worked. Undoubtedly her books suffered. She has written nothing that is likely to live, but here and there we find in her work passages of a lofty tone which prove that she had the power under favourable circumstances to have produced a really great book.

Of the other two or three novelists referred to, Mrs Henry Wood (1814—1887) by her *East Lynne* gained a remarkable hold upon the lovers of sensation, while Dinah Maria Craik (1826—1887) by her *John Halifax, Gentleman*, caught the fancy of the more sober-minded. *East Lynne* has no small share of the merits and faults of Lord Lytton's work. It is Mrs Wood's best book; but her pen was very prolific and the readers of the sixties counted upon her for a new novel yearly in her magazine *The Argosy*. *The Heir of Redclyffe* is another famous book of the same period. It was written by Charlotte Mary Yonge (1823—1901) who supplied the light literature which schoolgirls read half a century ago. The author of *The Daisy Chain*, *The Chaplet of Pearls*, etc. might be passed over unnamed but for the esteem in which *The Heir of Redclyffe* was held by the young Oxford school of the time. One of them, who was associated with the Pre-Raphaelites, has spoken of it as "unquestionably one of the greatest books in the world," and men so great as Burne Jones, William Morris and Rossetti seem to have been warm admirers. At the present day we can only note the fact and wonder. The world has been content to forget one of its greatest books, and when the pages are opened now they seem weak and sentimental.

§ 5. *Contemporaries of Dickens and Thackeray*

From the immense heap of novels which were written in the latter half of the nineteenth century it is possible to pick out a few which may indicate the spirit of the age. The easily-written tales of Sir Walter Scott were succeeded by historical novels which the writers took very seriously. George Eliot went to Florence to study old documents in order to supply herself with the materials for *Romola*; Charles Kingsley read all that he could find about Egyptian learning in order to write his story of *Hypatia*; and Charles Reade ransacked the libraries for documents bearing upon the Protestant Reformation before he began *The Cloister and the Hearth.* The author of the Waverley Novels had a much more direct and simple method. When he had not a suitable incident he invented one, and when his critics pointed out mistakes, he smiled and directed their attention to others which they had not noticed.

The spirit which insists upon fidelity in historical novels is a phase of what is known as realism; but the taste it indicates, which was characteristic of this period of the nineteenth century, was more easily gratified in another way than by the historical novel. The natural response to it was the novel of contemporary life; and this is the species of novel which chiefly prevailed during the years about which we are writing. There were endless varieties of the species—sentimental, romantic, comic, sarcastic, psychological, religious. But there was one variety, the novel of purpose, so important and so comprehensive that it requires special notice. No type of novel has been the subject of more discussion. It is anathema to the devotees of "art for art's sake." But in reality it is good or bad, not in itself, but according as the purpose is worked out. The valid objection is not to the presence of purpose, but to making character and artistic beauty subservient to the purpose. Undoubtedly this is a temptation which besets the novelist of purpose, and there are instances in the works of Dickens, Reade and others, in which the temptation has not been resisted.

Charles Reade (1814—1884) was the son of an Oxfordshire squire, and, though he was never wealthy, his private income and his fellowship, and finally his position of Vice-President of Magdalen College, Oxford, exempted him from the need to write in order to live. He was a briefless barrister, a most kind and generous though pugnacious man, but one who was absolutely wanting in self-knowledge. He set out to be a dramatist, and after he had produced thirteen plays which no manager would venture to put upon the stage he still obstinately refused to recognise failure and try his powers elsewhere. "Why don't you write novels?" asked his friend Mrs Seymour the actress, after he had read her a scene from one of those dramas which nobody would act. She saw where his real gifts lay, and her judgment is confirmed by the fact that Reade's most successful plays were written in collaboration. One of them is *Masks and Faces*, in which Reade's fellow-worker, Tom Taylor, was one of the most popular play-wrights of his time. At the age of thirty-nine Reade yielded to necessity and turned to the novel, though he did not abandon the drama. The ambition he still cherished is indicated by the inscription which he directed to be put upon his tombstone. There he is described as "dramatist, novelist, journalist." Thus the first place is given to the art in which he had most ambition to achieve fame, rather than to that in which he won it.

Reade's great maxim was never to guess where he could know; and at whatever trouble or cost to himself he acted on this principle. When he wanted fisher-folk for his novel *Christie Johnstone*, although he was a severe sufferer from sea sickness, he would not content himself with studying the fishermen on shore, but frequently accompanied them on their fishing expeditions. And although in youth he had given up his idea of being a doctor because of his shrinking from the sight of blood, he lamented missing the sight of a fatal accident, because he was convinced that no description could ever give him the vividness of a direct impression. He was never tired of repeating that "truth is stranger than fiction"; and he took so much pains to discover what the facts were that it is dangerous to challenge his most surprising statements. But whether he was altogether wise may be doubted. He never knew the profound truth of Stevenson's saying, "the actual is not true." Stevenson meant that truth of fact is not always the same as artistic truth. And Reade, though he can quote chapter and verse in support of the most unusual occurrences in his novels, has told stories which sometimes "affect us as a lie." Nevertheless his careful accumulation of human documents has given weight and solidity to his novels, and his skilful use of his materials will make them wear well.

Reade's long persistence in dramatic work, the great preparations he considered necessary for his stories, and the various lawsuits in which he found himself engaged swallowed up so much of life that his total output of books is not large. *It is Never Too Late to Mend* was the first of his books to win a great success. It is a picture of gaol life drawn from an inspection of several prisons, and among them the very Reading gaol which has been immortalised by Oscar Wilde's poem, *The Ballad of Reading Gaol.* Reade's novel had for its object the reformation of prison discipline. Eden, the prison reformer, is an intensely interesting man, and Susan Morton is one of the best of Reade's female characters. *Hard Cash,* a story much less attractive than *It is Never Too Late to Mend,* is intended to expose the abuses of lunatic asylums. *Griffith Gaunt,* with jealousy as its leading vice, drew down much unfavourable criticism; but the subject which Shakespeare handled in *Othello* has surely a right to artistic treatment. There was more cause to object in the case of *A Terrible Temptation.*

But none of these works of Reade contains characters or creations equal to the husband-monk Gerard, and his beautiful wife Margaret Brandt, in *The Cloister and the Hearth*. This book is one of the greatest of English novels. Its theme, as the name suggests, is the struggle between religion on the one hand, and the claims of a home on the other. The scene is laid in the fifteenth century. Few writers could have filled a canvas so extraordinarily large; but Reade is completely successful, and the interest in the story never flags.

Next perhaps in importance to Reade, among the men who were social reformers as well as novelists, was Charles Kingsley (1819—1875), a man of multifarious activity—professor of history at Cambridge, parson and poet, as well as novelist. But though he wrote some fine lyrics, and though there are some who hold that *The Saint's Tragedy* is his greatest production, it is for his works in prose fiction that he is best remembered. The majority of them fall under the head either of novels of purpose or of historical romances. To the former class belong *Yeast* and *Alton Locke*, which are among the best expositions of what was then known as Christian Socialism. They were written under the influence of Carlyle, and, unlike Reade's novels of purpose, are rather attacks upon the whole social system than assaults upon particular abuses. One of the favourite doctrines of Kingsley was that the working man who raised himself above his class was a traitor to it. He could see no possibility of permanent improvement in any class, if the best always moved into the next higher. This theory, applied with thorough-going consistency, would result in a system of caste. Such an outcome was far from the thoughts of Kingsley. He was fiery in his indignation over the wrongs and distress of the labouring classes and eager to find a way of helping them. Kingsley's best known novels are *Westward Ho!* and *Hereward the Wake*. Both are more pleasing to boys than to men. They tell thrilling stories of the sailors of

Queen Elizabeth and of the Vikings' sons. The story of *Hypatia* is laid in the time when Alexandria was the centre of society and of learning. *The Water Babies* belongs to no time. It is an exquisite fairy tale, the outcome of Kingsley's love for nature and for young things. This spontaneous expression of his sensitiveness to the charm of outdoor life is perhaps the best of all his works.

Another novelist who touched his high-water mark in writing for the young is Thomas Hughes (1823—1896), the author of *Tom Brown's School Days*. This book gives the best picture we have of Rugby School under the mastership of Arnold. Hughes makes no plot, while plot was the speciality of Wilkie Collins (1824—1889), the best of English novelists in what R. L. Stevenson calls "the art of carpentry" in fiction. In this respect his *Moonstone* is perhaps unequalled, and his *Woman in White* is very good.

Anthony Trollope (1815—1882) was a man of much greater calibre. From his earliest days he meant to be a novelist, but his mother, who was herself a writer of fiction, made him instead a clerk in the Post Office. When he wrote his first story, *The Macdermots of Ballycloran*, she prophesied its failure without prejudicing her mind by reading it. The immediate result seemed to justify her. For ten years Trollope had no success, and then *The Warden* brought him £9. 2*s*. 6*d*. by its first year's sale.

No effort is needed to read Trollope's books and none went to their making. Their author held that the man of letters had no more right than the village shoemaker to pause in his work for "inspiration." To him production of stories was automatic, and when one was completed he started another with the same rapidity as his fellow craftsman the worker in leather. All the tales belonging to his best series are laid in Barsetshire, a county which he created, giving it railways, roads, rivers, villages, and in his novels musing upon its growth or decay as if it had been the route of his daily walk. His clerical novels are his greatest triumph, yet, when he located his cathedral city and filled up the houses of the Dean's yard with their ecclesiastical inhabitants, Trollope had never lived in a cathedral city, London excepted, nor was he on familiar terms even with a curate. Among the clerical novels are the six which begin with *The Warden* and end with *The Last Chronicle of Barset*. *Can You Forgive Her? Phineas Finn* and *The Prime Minister* belong to another group, whose special interest lies in the fact that in them Trollope makes a deliberate attempt to trace the process of development in character, and to show how it is affected by change of circumstances and by the lapse of years. But he was less at ease with the Duke of Omnium than he was with the folk in Dean's yard. His natural atmosphere is that of the professional classes, the squires and the parsons. He deals with everyday life. His biggest sensation is a clerical squabble in the Cathedral yard, or a curtain lecture from Mrs Proudie, the bishop's wife. Yet we find ourselves reading the frank, pleasant stories again and again with increasing satisfaction. His own criticism of *Framley Parsonage* gives as sound an estimate of his work as can be written: "The story was thoroughly English," he says. "There was a little fox-hunting, and a little tuft-hunting, some Christian virtue and some Christian cant. There was no heroism and no villainy. There was much church, but more love-making."

§ 6. *George Meredith*

While Trollope was at the height of his fame George Meredith, whose work as a poet has already been treated, was known only to a very few, and even to this small circle of readers he was a puzzle. His first important story, the curious eastern tale *The Shaving of Shagpat*, was pronounced by George Eliot to be "a work of genius and of poetical genius," and declared to be "a new Arabian Night." Four years after *Shagpat* came what many now regard as his greatest novel, *The Ordeal of Richard Feverel.* Nevertheless it was nineteen years before the public asked for a second edition. In this book we have the famous chapter entitled Ferdinand and Miranda, one of the most fascinating love-scenes in literature; and Mark Twain in his inimitable Tom Sawyer does not surpass Meredith in his picture of the boys Richard and Ripton, nor show more complete understanding of the ludicrous stratagems of boy-nature. The character of Sir Austin in this book is one of Meredith's masterpieces. He is an egoist—a favourite subject of the author. There is Sir Austin, who feels that he, not Providence, sits at the seat of government, and Sir Willoughby Patterne, a companion portrait in *The Egoist*, who leans upon his fifty thousand a year, and expects thereby to come to terms with whom he will. We watch them both wreck their own lives and the lives of those dependent upon them by reason of their overweening self-confidence. Clara Middleton, the girl who grew tired of the selfish folly of Sir Willoughby, ranks with Diana of the Crossways among the finest of Meredith's women. The description of her hair is one of the novelist's exquisite pieces of word-painting—"This way and that the little lighter-coloured irreclaimable curls running truant from the comb and the knots—curls, half curls, root curls, vine ringlets, wedding rings, fledgling feathers, tufts of down, blown wisps—waved or fell, waved over or up or involutedly, loose and downward, in the form of small silken paws, hardly any of them much thicker than a crayon shading, cunninger than long round locks of gold to trick the heart."

Diana of the Crossways is perhaps Meredith's most widely read book. Its heroine is believed to be a portrait of the Honourable Mrs Norton. Meredith, like Thackeray, preferred to take his characters from the upper ranks of society. We have, it is true, in *Evan Harrington* the story of a tailor's son, but the book is partly family history and the hero is always wanting to forget the trade from which he has sprung. *Rhoda Fleming* is the only book which finds its chief interest among the yeoman class, and even in it the reader feels that the heroines Rhoda and especially Dahlia are princesses in disguise.

Meredith's power of drawing female characters is very remarkable. Except George Eliot he had no rival among contemporary writers, and she had the advantage of possessing a woman's soul and heart. But Meredith's imagination gave him the key; and his extraordinary sympathy gave him the light by which to understand the workings of the human mind. Oscar Wilde said "he had mastered every thing but language." The answer is possible, that it remains for readers to learn his speech; Goethe suggests somewhere that we can only see that which we are educated to see. There is no doubt Meredith delighted in playing pranks with his style, for after he inherited the legacy which gave him partial independence he says, "I took it into my head to serve these gentlemen (the critics) a strong dose of my most indigestible production." The packet labelled "indigestible" contained among other things *One of our Conquerors* and *The Amazing Marriage.* In the latter book the character of Woodseer is meant to be a partial portrait of R. L. Stevenson.

§ 7. *Other Story-Tellers*

There is no kinship between Meredith and the group of miscellaneous story-tellers now to be considered. They are so varied in their methods and aims that they can hardly be gathered together under any definite name. Chronologically the first is George MacDonald (1824—1905).

He was a descendant of the Highland clan who came to their tragic end in the pass of Glencoe, and when there was an opening he did not forget to recall the cruel wrongs of his race. He was born in Aberdeenshire, and did for that bleak corner of Scotland what Mrs Gaskell did for Lancashire and Mr Barrie has done for Kirriemuir. In his early life MacDonald was a preacher. For a time he was minister of a congregational church at Arundel; but his teaching was not of the kind approved by his flock, and he had to resign. In the field of literature, to which he then gave himself up, he never ceased to be a moral teacher, and every page he wrote bears witness to his sincerity and faith. *Robert Falconer* is his best novel. In general, his stories of Scotland are better than those of which the scene is laid in England. In the latter country his genius grows dim and we miss the full free expression of his Celtic spirit.

Much of this spirit is to be found in *The Sin Eater* and other books of Highland superstition written by William Sharp (1856—1905) under the pseudonym of Fiona Macleod. Sharp wrote also under his own name, and was a poet of considerable merit as well as a writer of fiction. As William Sharp he must be ranked among the Neo-Pre-Raphaelites; as Fiona Macleod he is a writer of the Celtic Revival. The two phases together in the same individual present one of the most interesting and puzzling of literary problems. How are we to explain the profound knowledge of the Highland Celt shown by the Lowlander, a native of the prosaic industrial town of Paisley, and his perfect sympathy with the life and feelings and language of another race[1]? Sharp's own answer was that it was a case of dual personality. The works published under the name of Fiona Macleod were written by a spirit at once Celtic and, as the

[1] Perhaps, however, this is only the judgment of the Saxon. There are Gaels who cannot abide Fiona Macleod.

name suggests, feminine. Whatever is the explanation, there is in the Fiona Macleod stories something far more profoundly Celtic than merely the broken English of the characters of another Lowland novelist, William Black.

In the twenty years or so during which the fame of Trollope was at its height the novel of manners was predominant. But other tastes continued to exist, and the most important thing now to notice is the reappearance of romance as the vogue of the story of manners passed away. William Black illustrates one phase of this new romance, and other aspects are to be seen in the novels of Richard Blackmore, of Besant and Rice, and, above all, in those of R. L. Stevenson.

Richard Blackmore (1825—1900) deserves to be remembered as the author of one of the best historical romances of the last half-century, the Devonshire story of *Lorna Doone.* Walter Besant (1836—1901) and James Rice (1843—1882) wrote nothing worthy to be set beside *Lorna Doone.* But although he wrote also *The Maid of Sker* Blackmore may be called a man of one book, while they are the writers of many pleasant stories. To something of the merits of Trollope, though on a lower plane, they add something of the charm of romance brought into relation with everyday life. They afford a remarkable example of literary partnership, for, down to the death of Rice, their novels were joint productions. Their partnership resembles the relation between two much greater men, Beaumont and Fletcher. Among the works written by Besant alone *All Sorts and Conditions of Men* deserves mention, for it turned the attention of men to East London, as perhaps it had never been turned before, and the People's Palace is a memorial of its influence.

Contemporary with Besant was the semi-mystical writer Joseph Henry Shorthouse (1834—1903), a Quaker who changed his simple faith for high Anglicanism. His books give the impression that they were written by a student in a college or cloister; but they were the work of an active man of business and were penned in the midst of bustling modern Birmingham. Shorthouse gave up his leisure for ten years to *John Inglesant*, which appeared in 1881, the same year as Stevenson's *Virginibus Puerisque.* But except for studied beauty of style there is no point of contact between the two novelists.

Samuel Butler (1835—1902) was, like Shorthouse, an isolated figure. His two best known works, *Erewhon; or Over the Range* and *Erewhon Revisited*, belong to the class of which *Gulliver's Travels* is the greatest example in English. But Butler was always alone in thought, and the two works named have a depth of foundation which no other modern architect of imaginary societies has reached. Still greater is *The Way of all Flesh.*

George Gissing (1857—1903) can likewise easily be classed; but he too, in respect of what he has done best, stands alone. He is one of the writers who have chosen for their principal theme the bare and ugly life to which modern industrialism has condemned the majority in England. Probably Gissing could have justified his harshest scenes; but the work of Dickens, of whom Gissing was one of the best and most appreciative critics, suggests a reason why the justification would be incomplete. Dickens saw the joyousness of the poor as well as their privations; Gissing saw only their privations. But the work by which Gissing deserves to live in literature is something wholly different—the exquisite *Private Papers of Henry Ryecroft.* If we could be sure that reward would always be commensurate with merit, the prophecy might be ventured that this beautiful piece of spiritual autobiography will become one of the classics of the English language.

§ 8. *R. L. Stevenson*

By far the greatest figure amongst these later romance writers is Robert Louis Stevenson (1850—1894), who, though intended by nature for a man of letters, was born into a family of engineers and destined by his people for their profession. His whole life was a gallant struggle against ill-health. The fight began in his babyhood, when in the long dreary night, between the paroxysms of coughing, his nurse would hold him up to look into the dark street and over to the light in another sick chamber, and he and she would wonder if there was another little boy aching like him, and wearily waiting there for morning. It was a deep grief to his father when Louis refused to follow the family profession and declared himself unable to accept the family religion. The breach between them widened when at a later time he determined to marry Mrs Osbourne, an American lady whose acquaintance he had made at Fontainebleau. He cut the knot of difficulties by sailing for San Francisco and making her his wife. There is no doubt that she was, in his own words, "made to be his mate." But to win her Stevenson had to struggle through desperate poverty, ill-health and painful domestic quarrels. "Here is a good heavy cross with a vengeance," he writes with reference to these disputes, "and all rough with rusty nails that tear your fingers, only it is not I that have to carry it alone; I hold the light end, but the heavy burden falls on these two." Peace was restored in 1880, when his father allowed him an income of £250 and admitted that he had judged his son's wife too harshly. Stevenson, as he said himself, could not live in an English climate, he could only die, so he and his wife set up their home in the South Sea islands. "Keep him alive," the doctor said, "till he is forty, and then, although a winged bird, he may live till he is ninety." He died at forty-four. He had lived fourteen years in the South Seas. After his death the Samoans passed in procession beside his bed in the great hall of his Vailima home. They knelt to him, their dead chief Tusitala, and kissed his hand.

Stevenson had not the appearance of a Briton, and least of all of a Scot. In his *Inland Voyage* he says, "I might come from any part of the globe, it seems, except from where I do." In France he was taken for a Frenchman; he has recorded his imprisonment as a German spy; and at a later date he writes, "I have found out what is wrong with me—I look like a Pole." Yet in the *Vailima Letters* which he wrote home from the South Seas, he laments that he cannot die in Scotland and be "buried in the hills under the heather, and a table tombstone like the martyrs, where the whaups and plovers are crying." He made voyages with his father round the lighthouses of the northern seas, and in his boyhood he lay amidst the purple heather of the high moorlands, smelling its blossoms, and listening to the cry of the whaup. He is at his best when he writes of Scotch things and Scotch people. He loved the land of his birth. "Singular," he says, "that I should fulfil the Scot's destiny throughout, and live a voluntary exile, and have my head filled with the blessed beastly place all the time."

The first book which brought Stevenson fame was *Treasure Island.* In it he used his knowledge of the seas and the thrilling possibilities of wrecks, and rock caves, and deserted islands, and hidden treasure. He raised a boy's book into a story captivating to all ages. *The Strange Case of Dr Jekyll and Mr Hyde* belongs to another order of writing. Stevenson dreamt this story of a dual personality, and wrote it off at red heat as it had been presented to him in his sleep. *Kidnapped* deals with Scotland and its history just after the battle of Culloden. Though it cannot touch the Waverley Novels in sweep and breadth and variety, it is the best story of the kind since Scott. Its sequel *Catriona* falls short of *Kidnapped*, but it has a feminine element, which the latter book has not. *The Master of Ballantrae* comes between these two in quality as well as date. *St Ives*, a tale of a French prisoner of war, which Stevenson left unfinished, was completed with great skill by Sir Arthur Quiller Couch. *Weir of Hermiston*, another fragment, is Stevenson's greatest work. It stands gloomy and grand, an unhewn rock with infinite possibilities. The brutality of the old judge, his powerful intellect and the cruelty of his justice combine to make the most wonderful character Stevenson has given us. We link this work with that of Emily Brontë, another genius who died young. Stevenson had an astonishing power of touching the heartstrings either to fear or sadness. On one occasion his sympathetic account of the hard lot of the legs of a chair, for ever supporting an idle seat, reduced a listening boy to the verge of tears. He made himself a great master of prose style. His touch was like that of Midas, only his pen turned everything into beauty, not into gold. He loved to linger over words and phrases, picking and choosing from all the wealth at his command, as a beautiful girl dallies with her trinket case. This continuous careful search for the best word was the outcome of his theory of the art of writing:—"There is," he says, "but one art—to omit! O if I knew how to omit I would ask no other knowledge. A man who knows how to omit would make an *Iliad* of a daily paper."

So far we have thought of Stevenson only as a writer of novels; but perhaps, had he not been pressed by circumstances to make money by his works, he would have written more poetry than the exquisite *Child's Garden of Verse* and its companion volume. And through his powerful imagination and his wide range of human interests, he might, had he had time to study the intricate art of stagecraft, have been more successful as a playwright.

§ 9. *Stories for Children*

It is a short step from the author of the most perfect modern book for boys to the delightful story-tellers who have enriched the children of the Victorian era. About nothing else is it so safe to repeat the boast of one of Homer's heroes, that we are much better than our fathers. The old nursery tales remain, it is true, unsurpassed; but they are an inheritance of the race, and the work of no one knows whom. If we limit ourselves to the authors of children's books who can be named, there are none equal to those who have arisen and written within the last half century or so. Three may be selected from among them for special honour; and first, because he is greatest, Charles Lutwidge Dodgson (1832—1898), better known as Lewis Carroll, the creator of *Alice's Adventures in Wonderland* and *Through the Looking-Glass*. Dodgson was a mathematician by profession, and no one looking at the learned old man sitting at the high table of Christ Church, Oxford, would have dreamed of his extensive acquaintance with fairies; yet in his early days he revealed his bent, making shows of dolls and marionettes, and wandering around in apparently close intimacy with snails, toads and all sorts of strange pets. There is a pretty story which throws a light upon his power of understanding the unseen. He made an appointment to meet a lady with a great gift for painting fairies. The spot selected was a crowded public place. When the lady arrived there she began to wonder how they were to know each other in the multitude. Presently a gentleman entered with two little girls clinging to his hands. He stooped and spoke to one, and then came at once to the lady. When she asked how he knew her, Lewis Carroll replied, "My little friend found you. I told her I had come to meet a young lady who knew fairies, and she fixed on you at once. But *I* knew you before she spoke."

Two other remarkable makers of children's books are Margaret Gatty (1809—1873) and her daughter Juliana Horatia Ewing (1841—1885). Mrs Gatty was the daughter of the Rev. A. J. Scott, Nelson's chaplain on board the *Victory*, and her first book was a collection of reminiscences of her father. The real work of her life however was her children's stories, initiated by *Fairy Godmothers and other Tales*. They were written partly from the suggestions of her brilliant little girl Juliana. Aunt Judy was her nursery nickname, and it gave the title to *Aunt Judy's Tales* and *Aunt Judy's Magazine*. Her daughter's books are more varied and finer. In *Madame Liberality* we see a portrait of Mrs Ewing herself. As a rule the little stories are domestic, and appeal to girls rather than to boys. But Mrs Ewing had a fairly wide range, and her *We and the World* is an admirable book for boys. She must have spun the adventure in it out of her own brain, for her delicate health kept her out of reach of any exciting occurrences. *The Land of Lost Toys*, *Jackanapes* and *Jan of the Windmill* are pieces of genuine literature, beautifully written, and firmly based on child-nature.

§ 1. *The Successors of Scott.*

Thomas Love Peacock, 1785—1866.
Headlong Hall, 1816.
Melincourt, 1817.
Nightmare Abbey, 1818
Maid Marian, 1822.
The Misfortunes of Elphin, 1829.
Crotchet Castle, 1831.
Gryll Grange, 1860.

Imitators of Scott.

William Harrison Ainsworth, 1805—1882.
Rookwood, 1834.
Jack Sheppard, 1839.
The Tower of London, 1840.
Old St Paul's, 1841.
Windsor Castle, 1843.
John Gibson Lockhart, 1794—1854.
Adam Blair, 1822.
John Galt, 1779—1839.
Annals of the Parish, 1821.
The Ayrshire Legatees, 1821.
The Entail, 1823.

Irish Writers.

William Carleton, 1794—1869.
The Pilgrimage to Lough Derg, 1828.
Traits and Stories of the Irish Peasantry, 1830—1833.
Fardorougha the Miser, 1837—1838.
Valentine McClutchy, 1845.
Parra Sastha, 1845.
The Emigrants of Ahadarra, 1847.
Willy Reilly, 1855.
Autobiography (in *Life* by D. J. O'Donoghue), 1896.
John Banim, 1798—1842.
Tales by the O'Hara Family (with Michael Banim), 1825—1827.
Gerald Griffin, 1803—1840.
The Collegians, 1829.

William Maginn, 1793—1842.
Francis Mahony, 1804—1866.
Reliques of Father Prout, 1834—1836.
T. Crofton Croker, 1798—1854.
Fairy Legends and Traditions of the South of Ireland, 1825.
Samuel Lover, 1797—1868.
Handy Andy, 1842.
Charles Lever, 1806—1872.
Harry Lorrequer, 1839.
Charles O'Malley, 1841.
Tom Burke of Ours, 1844.
Tony Butler, 1865.
Sir Brook Fossbrooke, 1866.

Novelists of War and of Sea.

James Grant, 1822—1887.
The Romance of War, 1845.
Frederick Marryat, 1792—1848.
Peter Simple, 1834.
Jacob Faithful, 1834.
Japhet in Search of a Father, 1836.
Midshipman Easy, 1836.
Masterman Ready, 1841.

Lytton and Disraeli.

Edward Bulwer Lytton (Lord Lytton), 1803—1873.
Falkland, 1827.
Pelham, 1828.
Paul Clifford, 1830.
Eugene Aram, 1832.
The Last Days of Pompeii, 1834.
Rienzi, 1835.
Zanoni, 1842.
The Last of the Barons, 1843.
Harold, 1848.
The Caxtons, 1849.
My Novel, 1853.
What will He do with It? 1859.
The Coming Race, 1871.
Kenelm Chillingly, 1873.

Benjamin Disraeli (Earl of Beaconsfield), 1804—1881.
Vivian Grey, 1826—1827.
The Young Duke, 1831.
Contarini Fleming, 1832.
The Wondrous Tale of Alroy, 1833.
Venetia, 1837.
Henrietta Temple, 1837.
Coningsby, 1844.
Sybil, 1845.
Tancred, 1847.
Lothair, 1870.
Endymion, 1880.

§ 2. *Dickens.*

Charles Dickens, 1812—1870.
Sketches by Boz, 1836.
The Pickwick Papers, 1836—1837.
Oliver Twist, 1837—1838.
Nicholas Nickleby, 1838—1839.
The Old Curiosity Shop, 1840—1841.
Barnaby Rudge, 1841.
Martin Chuzzlewit, 1843—1844.
Dombey and Son, 1846—1848.
David Copperfield, 1849—1850.
Bleak House, 1852—1853.
Hard Times, 1854.
Little Dorrit, 1855—1857.
A Tale of Two Cities, 1859.
Our Mutual Friend, 1864—1865.
The Mystery of Edwin Drood, 1870.

§ 3. *Thackeray.*

William Makepeace Thackeray, 1811—1863.
The Great Hoggarty Diamond, 1841.
Barry Lyndon, 1844.
Vanity Fair, 1847—1848.
The Book of Snobs, 1848 (in *Punch*, 1846—1847).
Pendennis, 1849—1850.
The English Humourists of the Eighteenth Century, 1851.
Esmond, 1852.
The Newcomes, 1853—1855.

The Four Georges, 1855—1866.
The Virginians, 1857—1859.
The Adventures of Philip, 1861.
Denis Duval, 1864.
George du Maurier, 1834—1896.
Trilby, 1894.

§ 4. *Women Novelists.*

Charlotte Brontë, 1816—1855.
Jane Eyre, 1847.
Shirley, 1849.
Villette, 1853.
The Professor, 1857.
Emily Brontë, 1818—1848.
Wuthering Heights, 1847.
Elizabeth Cleghorn Gaskell, 1810—1865.
Mary Barton, 1848.
Ruth, 1853.
Cranford, 1853.
North and South, 1855.
Sylvia's Lovers, 1863.
Cousin Phillis, 1865.
Wives and Daughters, 1866.
George Eliot, 1819—1880.
Scenes of Clerical Life, 1857.
Adam Bede, 1859.
The Mill on the Floss, 1860.
Silas Marner, 1861.
Romola, 1863.
Felix Holt, 1866.
Middlemarch, 1871—1872.
Daniel Deronda, 1876.
Mrs Henry Wood, 1814—1887.
East Lynne, 1861.
Dinah Maria Craik, 1826—1887.
John Halifax, Gentleman, 1856.
Charlotte Mary Yonge, 1823—1901.
The Heir of Redclyffe, 1853.
Margaret Oliphant, 1828—1897.
Margaret Maitland, 1849.
The Chronicles of Carlingford, 1863—1876.

§ 5. *Contemporaries of Dickens and Thackeray.*

Charles Reade, 1814—1884.
Peg Woffington, 1853.
Christie Johnstone, 1853.
It is Never Too Late to Mend, 1856.
The Cloister and the Hearth, 1861.
Hard Cash, 1863.
Griffith Gaunt, 1866.
Put Yourself in His Place, 1870.
A Terrible Temptation, 1871.
Charles Kingsley, 1819—1875.
Yeast, 1848.
The Saint's Tragedy, 1848.
Alton Locke, 1850.
Hypatia, 1853.
Westward Ho! 1855.
The Water Babies, 1863.
Hereward the Wake, 1866.
Thomas Hughes, 1822—1896.
Tom Brown's School Days, 1857.
Wilkie Collins, 1824—1889.
Antonina, 1850.
The Woman in White, 1860.
Armadale, 1866.
The Moonstone, 1868.
Anthony Trollope, 1815—1882.
The Macdermots of Ballycloran, 1847.
The Warden, 1855.
Barchester Towers, 1857.
Doctor Thorne, 1858.
The Three Clerks, 1858.
Framley Parsonage, 1861.
The Small House at Allington, 1864.
Can You Forgive Her? 1864.
The Last Chronicle of Barset, 1867.
Phineas Finn, 1869.
Phineas Redux, 1874.
The Prime Minister, 1876.
Autobiography, 1883.

§ 6. *George Meredith.*

George Meredith, 1828—1909.
The Shaving of Shagpat, 1855.
The Ordeal of Richard Feverel, 1859.
Evan Harrington, 1861.
Emilia in England (*Sandra Belloni*), 1864.
Rhoda Fleming, 1865.
Vittoria, 1866.
The Adventures of Harry Richmond, 1871.
Beauchamp's Career, 1876.
The Egoist, 1879.
The Tragic Comedians, 1880.
Diana of the Crossways, 1885.
One of our Conquerors, 1891.
The Amazing Marriage, 1895.

§ 7. *Other Story-Tellers.*

George MacDonald, 1824—1905.
David Elginbrod, 1863.
Alec Forbes, 1865.
Robert Falconer, 1868.
Malcolm, 1875.
The Marquis of Lossie, 1877.
Sir Gibbie, 1879.
William Sharp, 1855—1905.
The Sin Eater, 1895.
The Dominion of Dreams, 1899.
William Black, 1841—1898.
Richard Blackmore, 1825—1900.
Lorna Doone, 1869.
The Maid of Sker, 1872.
Walter Besant, 1836—1901.
Ready-Money Mortiboy (with James Rice, 1843—1882), 1872.
The Golden Butterfly (with Rice), 1876.
All Sorts and Conditions of Men, 1882.
The Children of Gibeon, 1886.
Joseph Henry Shorthouse, 1834—1903.
John Inglesant, 1881.
Sir Percival, 1886.

Samuel Butler, 1835—1902.
Erewhon, 1872.
Erewhon Revisited, 1901.
The Way of All Flesh, 1903.
George Gissing, 1857—1903.
Demos, 1886.
New Grub Street, 1891.
The Private Papers of Henry Ryecroft, 1903.

§ 8. *R. L. Stevenson.*

Robert Louis Stevenson, 1850—1894.
An Inland Voyage, 1878.
Virginibus Puerisque, 1881.
Familiar Studies of Men and Books, 1882.
New Arabian Nights, 1882.
Treasure Island, 1882.
The Strange Case of Dr Jekyll and Mr Hyde, 1886.
Kidnapped, 1886.
The Master of Ballantrae, 1889.
The Wrecker (with Mr Lloyd Osbourne), 1892.
Catriona, 1893.
Island Nights' Entertainments, 1893.
The Ebb Tide (with Mr Lloyd Osbourne), 1894.
Weir of Hermiston, 1896.
St Ives, 1899.
In the South Seas, 1900.

§ 9. *Stories for Children.*

Charles Lutwidge Dodgson (Lewis Carroll), 1832—1898.
Alice's Adventures in Wonderland, 1865.
Through the Looking-Glass, 1871.
Margaret Gatty, 1809—1873.
Fairy Godmothers, and other Tales, 1851.
Aunt Judy's Tales, 1859.
Juliana Horatia Ewing, 1841—1885.
The Land of Lost Toys, 1869.
Madame Liberality, 1873.
Jan of the Windmill, 1876.
We and the World, 1877—1879.
Jackanapes, 1879.

CHAPTER IV

THE HISTORIANS

§ 1. *The Revolution in the Writing of History*

GREAT as is the difference between the poetry of the school of Pope and that of the poets of the later romance movement, it is not greater than, perhaps it is hardly as great as, that between the historians of the eighteenth century and those of the nineteenth. In history however the transition was somewhat later in showing itself. By 1760 there were numerous signs of change in poetry; but at that date Hume's *History* was still unfinished, and Robertson had written only one of the three works which made his reputation. In the early part of the nineteenth century these two, with Gibbon, were still among the authors whom "no gentleman's library should be without." Half a century later, so great had been the change of feeling that Huxley, in one of the best books ever written about Hume, passed over the famous *History of England* without criticism. It is not easy to say what caused such a profound change of opinion, but one or two suggestions towards an answer may be made. In the first place, the idea of nationality is prominent in the work of the nineteenth century; and it is interesting to notice that the *Decline and Fall* of Gibbon, the one work of the eighteenth century which is still accepted, is just that into which, from the nature of the subject, the question of nationality scarcely enters. Had his book dealt with a single people instead of the whole Roman Empire, it is doubtful whether even Gibbon's thoroughness would have made his treatment acceptable to the student of the present day. The French Revolution had intervened, with its assertion of the right of every nation to be itself, and mediæval conceptions of a universal empire were antiquated.

Again, science had to be reckoned with. The idea of evolution has been applied to history, and the student is almost as much interested in what a nation has come from as in what it has now become. Hume and his contemporaries did not care to study the rude customs or institutions of barbarians. They thought that only civilised men were worthy of attention. But the historical evolutionist is as much interested in crude beginnings as the biologist is in protoplasm.

Connected with this idea is the profound reverence for fact in modern history. In this respect history has been most deeply and directly indebted to science; and it is here perhaps that we find the real dividing line between the new school of history and the old. There can be no dispute as to the value of the modern method; but it is worth while to notice, because it is frequently forgotten, that, important as the spirit of research is, it may become misleading. To its influence must be ascribed the doctrine that history is a science pure and simple. And yet obviously human character is the raw material from which history is made; and no one has yet formulated a science of human character. Further, the modern method seems to have begotten a tendency to over-value facts as facts. The modern historian is like the millionaire who is worried with the custody of wealth which is too great for any man to use. The one is a slave to nis gold, the other to his facts. The task of a perfect historian would be to re-think the thoughts as well as to record the actions of those who have made history. These are not merely soldiers and statesmen but all mankind; and the most colossal mass of "hard facts" goes only a very little way towards the accomplishment of the task.

§ 2. *Students of the Origins*

The new interest in the beginnings of things is seen in the study of old English and of the early English as a people. Among the pioneers of this sort of learning was Sharon Turner (1768—1847), whose *History of the Anglo-Saxons* paved the way for subsequent writers. J. M. Kemble (1807—1857) followed him with *The Saxons in England.* Sir Francis Palgrave (1788—1861), a Deputy Keeper of the Records, was another pioneer, whose chief work was his *History of Normandy and of England.* Freeman declared of him that, as the discoverer of the fact that the Roman Empire did not end in 476 A.D., he deserved a place among the foremost of historians.

In the study of language and literature there was a movement similar to that which has been noticed in history. For the eighteenth century English literature began with *The Canterbury Tales*, and history, it may almost be said, with the Norman Conquest; but the men of the nineteenth century pushed the beginnings back by centuries. Kemble translated *Beowulf*, and Joseph Bosworth wrote a grammar and compiled a dictionary of the Anglo-Saxon language. Richard Chenevix Trench (1807—1886) investigated the language at a later stage, and wrote those attractive volumes, *On the Study of Words* and *English Past and Present*, which have done more than any other books to spread a knowledge of the history of English.

Philology however is a science which was "made in Germany." It was Grimm who inspired the earlier workers, and in later days the chief honours fell to a countryman of Grimm, Friedrich Max Müller (1823—1900) who, coming to England in 1846, learned to speak and write English with a grace and elegance never surpassed by any man of foreign birth.

Max Müller devoted himself to the science of comparative philology. His domain was the whole of human speech, but especially the Aryan family of languages, and, above all, Sanskrit. Besides this he was an authority upon comparative mythology and on the origin and growth of religions. So wide was his fame that when the people of Japan wanted a new religion they sent their envoys to Max Müller; and it is in their University of Tokio that the library which he collected has found its final home. He had a remarkable capacity for discovering the right thing to do and the right moment to do it. For instance, when war broke out with Russia a few years after he had settled in England, he had ready at once the book entitled *Languages of the Seat of War in the East.* To the end this power never failed him. Scholars did not understand this kind of tact, and they doubted the depth of a learning so wide and varied, and the sincerity of one who was gifted with the power of charming all sorts and conditions of men. But this versatility of mind has not put him outside the group of scientific historians, if a form of knowledge so varied and irreducible to law as the history of the human race ever can be studied on the same principles as science.

§ 3. *Ancient History*

The department of ancient history was the first to feel deeply the influence of this so-called scientific method. In the early years of the nineteenth century the chief authority on Greek history was Mitford; and with regard to Roman history the early legends were still largely accepted as records of literal facts. To minds in this state the work of German scholars like Niebuhr came as a revelation.

Niebuhr's merits were indeed exaggerated. Freeman says that his followers "avowedly claimed for him a kind of power of 'divination.'" But authority of this sort is never lasting, and that of Niebuhr was undermined, in England, by Sir George Cornewall Lewis's *Inquiry on the Credibility of Early Roman History*.

The three men by whom, or under whose influence, the history of Greece and Rome was rewritten were Thomas Arnold (1795—1842), Connop Thirlwall (1797—1875) and George Grote (1794—1871). It is however as head of Rugby School that Arnold will be best remembered. When he went from the quiet rectory of Laleham to Rugby, it ranked only among the second-class public schools of England, and not particularly high among these. When he died, it stood first of all. What he set himself to accomplish was not merely to give his pupils learning, but to mould their characters and to give them his own high conception of public and private duty. Arnold still lives also as a man of letters by his *History of Rome*; for, though much of his work has been superseded by the later researches of the German Mommsen, not to speak of lesser scholars, his histories of campaigns are admitted by military men to show the insight of a soldier, and they have a literary charm rarely found in the writing of men of action. Yet style was never Arnold's primary interest. His first consideration in writing was the thing to be said, and never the manner of saying it. His early writings are therefore sometimes clumsy and crude; but they have the power to convince which belongs to a man who knows his subject. His great object was to teach principles. He would not have thought it worth while to re-tell the story of ancient Rome if he had not believed that it was a practical subject by which he might teach political principles to English statesmen and citizens.

The other two historians, Thirlwall and Grote, had been

friends and schoolfellows, and now they rest in the same grave in Westminster Abbey; but, strangely enough, they knew nothing of one another's researches until the result began to appear in print. Of the two, Thirlwall was the profounder scholar; but he was unfortunate in the plan of his history, which was originally written for *Lardner's Cyclopaedia* and shows a want of proportion owing to the subsequent change of design.

Grote devoted far more time to Greek history than Thirlwall, and therefore, though the latter is the finer writer and the more impartial judge, the former, as the more thorough worker, on the whole surpassed his rival. Grote was stirred up to write his *History* by the extreme Toryism shown by Mitford in his *History of Greece*. In his desire to defend democracy he swung too far in the opposite direction. He is blind to the most obvious faults in the government of democratic Athens, and quite forgets that a democracy resting on slavery is not, in the modern sense, a democracy at all. It is therefore unsafe to assume, as he does, that a lesson may be drawn directly from ancient democracy for the use of modern democracy.

There is one other historian of the Greeks who deserves more than a passing mention. This is George Finlay (1799—1875) whom Freeman speaks of as "the most truly original historian of our time and language"; while J. S. Mill said that a page of him was worth a chapter of Gibbon. Finlay wrote *The History of Greece from its Conquest by the Romans to the Present Time*, that is, from 146 B.C. to 1864 A.D. It was not published until after his death. Finlay was not a great writer, nor is his *History* a work of art, but he was an enthusiast for his subject. He took part in the Greek war of independence, and for two months was in close association with Byron, leaving Missolonghi just nine days before the poet's death. After the end of the war he bought an estate, and settled in Greece.

Thenceforward till his death the greater part of his life was spent among the people whose cause he had espoused and whose history he was studying.

Finlay traced one line of connexion between the ancient and modern worlds, and Henry Hart Milman (1791—1868) made it his business in later life to trace another. He was at one time professor of poetry at Oxford, and up to 1829, when his *History of the Jews* appeared, his name had only been associated with poetry and plays. R. Garnett speaks of his history as "epoch-making." It certainly was startling to orthodox England, so startling that Milman's publisher found himself obliged to stop the series in which the *History* was appearing. Milman was accused of want of reverence for the scriptures, because he referred to Abraham as a sheik, and ventured to criticise the miracles. His promotion was stopped for a time by the outcry; but he was a man of rare courage and intellectual honesty, whom no ill treatment could induce to recant. The idea of treating the Jews with the same impartial investigation that we give to the annals of any other nation has now become so familiar to us that it is hard to appreciate what Milman did for freedom of thought. His later book, *The History of Latin Christianity, including that of the Popes to Nicholas V*, is his greatest and most ambitious work. He trained himself for it by his studies in Gibbon, whose history he edited and whose life he wrote. *The History of Latin Christianity* runs parallel with *The Decline and Fall.* Both works treat of the same period; and yet they are so widely different that, had Milman desired to emphasise the fact that he was not rewriting Gibbon, he might have done so by the use of the phrase "rise and progress." Gibbon writes of secular Rome, and tries to trace the causes of the decay of the worldly empire of the Caesars; Milman writes of Rome ecclesiastical and religious, and tries to trace the rise of the spiritual empire of the Popes.

The immense superiority of these historians of the ancient world to their predecessors naturally enough suggests the idea that they wrote history on some new method. But in reality the sole important difference is that they were more thorough and more conscientious than those whom they superseded.

§ 4. *Hallam and Macaulay*

It is however in the work of Henry Hallam (1777—1859) that we find the most direct link between the historical work of the eighteenth and nineteenth centuries. In *A View of the State of Europe during the Middle Ages* and *The Constitutional History of England*, he showed that readiness to undertake vast subjects which belongs to the earlier time; but with it he combined the power of research and the appreciation of old documents which characterise a more recent period. Time has considerably dimmed the reputation of the "judicious Hallam." The coldness and want of sympathy to which he owed this epithet do not conduce to human interest; and it has been discovered that his impartiality is marred and limited by the presence of certain preconceptions. It is difficult to understand that the man who wrote as Hallam wrote lived among men and women and was one of the most brilliant talkers in the famous society which gathered at Holland House; while the reason is evident why Macaulay described him as "a judge, but a hanging judge."

The historians who first exhibit the characteristics of the nineteenth century fully developed and on the great scale are Carlyle and Macaulay. But though they share the characteristics of their time they are widely different one from the other. "To reach the English intellect," says

Taine, "a Frenchman must make two voyages. When he has crossed the first interval, which is wide, he comes upon Macaulay. Let him re-embark; but he must accomplish a second passage, just as long, to arrive at Carlyle for instance,—a mind fundamentally Germanic, on the genuine English soil." Taine has not exaggerated the difference between these two men, or their importance. By reason of the wide influence Carlyle has exercised and exercises over all forms of thought, he has been treated in the first chapter. After him the highest place among the writers of history in the nineteenth century may be given to Thomas Babington Macaulay (1800—1859). He has been pronounced unsound and a prejudiced partisan; but Lord Acton, a very competent critic, speaks in terms of extraordinary warmth about his powers as a historian. A master in the art of writing pure vigorous English, Macaulay has never been found wanting in interest. His *Essays* have, probably more than any other book, brought multitudes to find entertainment in history.

The historian was the son of Zachary Macaulay, who surrendered the chance of opulence in order to devote himself to the cause of the West Indian slaves. In such a home Macaulay early learned to work for great causes and to be ready to sacrifice himself for the public good. He entered Cambridge a Tory, but was converted to Radicalism by Charles Austin, "the only man who ever dominated Macaulay." Ultimately he joined the Whigs and was the chief literary exponent of their principles. Besides Austin, John Moultrie, W. M. Praed, Henry Nelson Coleridge and Derwent Coleridge were among the brilliant group of Cambridge undergraduates in Macaulay's time. At college he was twice the winner of the prize for an English poem, and there too he began to write for *Knight's Quarterly Magazine*. As a student his passion for reading was notorious. It was in a sense a snare to him, and he indulged it to an extent which, in view of his astonishing memory, had not much meaning. He said that if *Paradise Lost* were destroyed he could repeat it from memory; yet he went on reading *Paradise Lost.* By this persistent re-reading of old favourites he may have become what he was, slow to admit a new author into favour, or to do justice to a fresh writer who broke away from convention. He thought less of Carlyle than of Addison; and the great wave of German influence hardly touched him.

It was shortly after he left college that Macaulay secured by his essay on Milton a connexion with the *Edinburgh Review* and won for himself a fame almost as dazzling and sudden as that which *Childe Harold* had gained for Byron. The famous *Critical and Historical Essays* were written for this periodical. In 1830 Macaulay entered parliament as a member for Calne. Four years later he accepted a seat on the supreme council for India. He spent four interesting years there, working strenuously to draft the Indian Penal Code, which, his biographer says, the "younger civilians now carry in their saddle bags and the older in their heads." When he returned to England he had saved sufficient money to enable him to devote himself to literature. He appeared again in parliament and became secretary at war. But he grudged the long hours passed in the House, and so, after his defeat at the election for Edinburgh in 1847, he resigned his office. Although he again sat in the House of Commons from 1852 till 1856, he no longer took any large part in political life. In the words of the fine lines he wrote when he was beaten at Edinburgh, he gave himself up to the Muse of literature, the "glorious Lady with the eyes of light," who had cheered the exile of Hyde, the captivity of Raleigh and the disgrace of Bacon. Two years before his death Macaulay was raised to the peerage as Baron Macaulay of Rothley.

In spirit and aim Macaulay was on one side akin to

the historians of the eighteenth century, and on the other to his contemporaries and successors of the nineteenth. Although his first venture in authorship took the form of criticisms and reviews, his work is mainly historical. He says himself, "I am nothing if not historical," and the truth of this judgment is impressed upon the reader at every page. He was what Lord Houghton very happily calls him, "a great historical orator and oratorical historian"; his essays might be very easily delivered as speeches, and his speeches read as essays. In his profound respect for facts he is in sympathy with the new school of history, but his wonderful skill in dressing them up, and making them no longer "hard," allies him with the older writers. He was a master of narrative and of the short crisp sentence so easily understood. He had at his command an enormous mass of details, and nothing was too trivial for him to use in order to make his picture more vivid. It is this that has made his *History* as interesting as a novel, and five times as long as it ought to be.

§ 5. *Froude*

The conception that a new method of writing history had been discovered, which is the product of a somewhat later time, gives rise to a conflict between two great schools, the literary and the so-called scientific. James Anthony Froude (1818—1894) is, after Carlyle and Macaulay, the best example of the literary school, while the scientific group is represented by William Stubbs (1825—1901), Edward Augustus Freeman (1823—1892), Samuel Rawson Gardiner (1829—1902), Mandell Creighton (1843—1901), and, partially, by John Richard Green (1837—1883).

Froude, who was the son of a clergyman, started life in a home that was too bigoted to admit into its library a copy of *The Pilgrim's Progress*. At Oxford, finding his brother Hurrell Froude hotly engaged in doing battle for the Tractarians, he too naturally fell under their influence, and was enlisted by Newman to write for *The Lives of the Saints*. When he was twenty-seven he was ordained deacon ; but his orthodoxy gave way before the time came for him to be a priest, and, as soon as the law permitted him, he cast off his clerical profession. His *Nemesis of Faith*, a sort of spiritual autobiography, came out while he was in orders. It caused great excitement. The senior tutor of Exeter College burned his copy (a borrowed one) in the hall of the College, and Froude had to resign his fellowship. He was even compelled to sell his books, for his father cut off the allowance of his heterodox son. Such was the penalty to be paid at that time for freedom of thought.

In the midst of these disasters Froude came across Carlyle, who speedily became the chief influence in his life. " If I wrote anything," he says, " I fancied myself writing it to him, reflecting at each word what he would think of it as a check on affectations." The first important work was begun at Carlyle's suggestion, and written in a great measure on Carlyle's conception of what history ought to be. In *The History of England from the Fall of Wolsey to the Defeat of the Spanish Armada* Froude set himself the task of telling the story of the Protestant Reformation, especially in England, and of showing by what means Protestantism finally became established as a ruling force over a great part of Europe. This was the reason why he stopped at 1588. He meant in his original plan to carry his history down to the death of Elizabeth, but he became convinced that the defeat of the Armada was the real Protestant triumph. In this work Froude displays one of his most notable gifts, the power of drawing character. It has been said that he has whitewashed Henry VIII and changed our conception of the whole Tudor family. It is quite certain that, though we may not fully accept his view of that family, he has permanently raised its reputation.

Several of Froude's minor works may be regarded as appendages to his *History*—for example, *The Divorce of Catharine of Aragon*, *The Spanish Story of the Armada* and *English Seamen in the Sixteenth Century*, but there are others which demand separate notice, because they are inspired by a new conception, the conception of imperialism. Froude visited the colonies, and from his visits came *Oceana*, *Lectures on South Africa* and *The English in the West Indies*. *The English in Ireland in the Eighteenth Century*, though it tells a different tale, is still animated by this imperialistic spirit. This idea, it is true, is present in the *History*, and was certainly strengthened in Froude's mind by his researches in writing that book; but that work is nevertheless mainly a history of the rise of Protestantism. The second group of books, on the other hand, are directly inspired by the idea of imperialism, and probably no other writer except Seeley has done more than Froude to foster this feeling among Englishmen.

An important work still to be noticed is his *Life of Carlyle*. In this Froude had a magnificent subject, and he has left behind one of the most fascinating of biographies. It is true he colours his characters too deeply and is inaccurate. Professor Norton calls *The Life of Carlyle* "a story founded on fact," and Mr David Wilson complains that in Froude's work there are as many errors as pages. Froude's inaccuracies and misstatements cannot be defended; but it is unfair to assert that he did not seek for the truth. He has received less than his due of credit for the original research he did for his *History*. He was the first Englishman to examine the great collection of documents at Simancas, and he laboured hard also at the documents in the Record Office. In Hatfield House, the residence of the Cecils, he found the sand which had been used to dry some manuscripts written centuries before glistening on the ink. This proved that his eye was the first to read the pages. Froude, by his conscientious research, and his unique power of presenting history to the reader in an interesting and beautiful form, has rendered a great service to students, a service which ought to be more generously estimated against his errors.

§ 6. *The Oxford Group*

To pass from the works of Froude to those of Freeman and Stubbs is to go into the new atmosphere of the Oxford school of historians, to which Froude, though he was an Oxford man, did not belong. Froude read widely for his work, but when he wrote he made few references. The men of the Oxford school on the other hand made constant reference to the original authorities a matter of conscience and duty. By this scrupulous zeal they gained for themselves a reputation for accuracy which caused them to be regarded by their admiring contemporaries as the superiors of all their predecessors. Now however men are more alive to their limitations and defects. Thus Freeman, owing to his aversion to using the British Museum and other great public libraries and his objection to authorities not in print, evidently cannot be said to have made use of all available documents. And, as will be seen later, his capricious temperament marred his judgment and drove him into assumptions which were not correct.

Until he was appointed regius professor of history at Oxford, Freeman spent most of his life in the country, whence he sent out a stream of articles chiefly historical, but sometimes dealing with such subjects as architecture and geography as they bore upon his special study. He published *The History and Conquest of the Saracens*, he began and left unfinished *The History of Federal Government*. But the great work of his life was *The*

History of the Norman Conquest and its sequel *The Reign of William Rufus.* In all his books he is prone to fall into certain characteristic mistakes. In his school days he learned from Arnold the idea of the unity of history. The conception was then novel, it was true to a certain extent, and it tended to demolish the old classifications of history into ancient and modern, secular and sacred. But Freeman insisted upon pushing the idea to the extreme. He underrated the importance of the deep lines of division which exist, though they do not completely break the connexion between the distant past and the present. There are, it is true, between the ancient world and the modern, many lines of connexion—through the law of Rome, through the literature and philosophy of Greece,—but it is none the less true that there is a wide difference between the ancient world and the modern. Freeman went so far as to oppose the use of modern history as a distinct subject of academic education, and argued against the proposal to establish a school of modern history in Oxford.

A similar prejudice is seen in Freeman's exaltation of the Teutons, and in his account of the conquest of the Celts. This account is almost pure theory, and further, it is singularly unconvincing theory. There is every reason, we are told, to believe that the Celtic inhabitants over a great part of England had been extirpated. Yet it is added that "the women would doubtless be largely spared," and that the men would have the alternatives of death, emigration or slavery. But if the women were spared there was no approach to extermination, even supposing that all the men chose the alternatives of death or emigration. Nor is Freeman's appeal to language more convincing. Nearly all the Welsh words which have survived in English express, he says, "some small domestic matter, such as women and slaves would be concerned with." And he draws the conclusion that in Britain, and, he admits, in Britain alone, "the intruding nation altogether supplanted the elder nation." But events which are unexampled ought to be established by the most rigorous evidence; and what Freeman adduces can hardly be called evidence at all.

The two ambitions of Freeman were to be a professor of history at Oxford, and to become a member of parliament. Towards the end of his life, when he had become too weary to care for honours, the chance of entering parliament was offered to him, but he declined it. He realised his other ambition, and became professor of history at Oxford. It is very rare for a professor at Oxford or Cambridge to be able to gather an audience, and few came to listen to Freeman's lectures. He was much disappointed, and pathetically wrote that he had tried every kind of lecture he could think of and had put his best strength into all, and nobody came. Probably he was himself to blame, for his writings do not show the qualities which make an attractive speaker. He never learned the art of omission; and the clumsy style in his ponderous books, with their dubious theories and unconvincing arguments, makes it extremely doubtful whether they will long continue to be read.

With the name of Freeman there is usually linked that of his friend William Stubbs. The two names naturally come together. The men were regarded as the most learned historians of their time, their aims and methods were alike, and their mutual admiration for each other was sometimes as diverting as it was profound. Thorold Rogers was awake to the amusing aspect of it, and wrote the well-known lines:

> "See, ladling butter from alternate tubs,
> Stubbs butters Freeman, Freeman butters Stubbs."

Stubbs was not only younger in years than his friend, but his work on the whole was later. It was both of a brighter character than Freeman's and more deeply learned.

Stubbs had an incisive manner of describing a character, and there is much lively and excellent writing in the introductions to the volumes of the Rolls series which he edited. This editorial work was executed in such a masterly way as to give the author a reputation so high that he was offered the Oxford professorship of history, for which he was not even a candidate. He held this post for eighteen years, when he was made Bishop of Chester. Two years later he was translated to Oxford, where the rest of his life was occupied in the administration of his diocese.

The selection of Stubbs to fill the chair of history in Oxford was fortunate, for it was during the years in which he held this position that he did his literary work. To that period belong *Select Charters*, *The Constitutional History of England*, *The Early Plantagenets* and *Lectures on the Study of Medieval and Modern History*, though he had become a bishop before the last was published.

The great interest in history for Stubbs lay on its ecclesiastical and constitutional sides, and his best known work is the *Constitutional History*. This and the histories on the same lines of Hallam and of May form a series of three books which together cover the whole course of English constitutional history from the beginning down to a time within living memory. Stubbs undertook the earliest period, tracing the constitutional history of England "in its origin and development."

The whole work of Stubbs is inspired with the conviction that the beginning is more than half the whole. He shares in a more moderate form the belief of Freeman that in substance almost the whole of our English laws were in use in Saxon times, and that recent changes are merely changes in detail. He did most important work, discovering much that was unknown, and putting much that was known in its proper place.

John Richard Green combined the brilliant writing of Macaulay with the method of his fellow-historians of the Oxford school. He started life as a curate in East London, where by his untiring zeal and hard work he sowed the seeds of the disease which doomed him to an early death. It was when forced by ill-health to retire from clerical life that he found leisure for his historical work. Like R. L. Stevenson he toiled bravely in face of death, working as best he could at health resorts, to which he had been driven by disease; like Stevenson too he was a brilliant talker and a fascinating letter-writer; and finally, like Stevenson he wrote his own epitaph—"he died learning."

A Short History of the English People pushed Green into fame at once. His enlargement of it into *A History of the English People* in four volumes has never taken so high a place in popular fancy as its smaller predecessor. His other books, *The Making of England* and *The Conquest of England*, were both written when he was practically under the shadow of death. They are the work of a true student, and, all things considered, it is astonishing how good they are. Green had a wonderful faculty for reviving the past. The colour of a robe or the description of a species of food would suggest to him a whole picture of domestic life amongst the Saxons. He saw at a glance the outstanding features in a historical landscape. It was he who made Freeman understand that a town in history is a real entity, with an important life of its own, and with records which will probably afford the key to valuable knowledge.

Mandell Creighton is another of the historians who did an important part of his work at Oxford. He was the contemporary of Green, but outlived him for nearly twenty years. He was for a considerable time fellow and tutor of an Oxford college, in which position he interested himself in the work of establishing the new school of modern history in the university. He also found leisure to publish

The Age of Elizabeth, *Simon de Montfort*, *The Tudors and the Reformation* and the first two volumes of *The History of the Papacy during the Period of the Reformation*, a title which became inaccurate when the author found that the pressure of other duties would prevent him from carrying the narrative farther down than the sack of Rome.

In its outstanding events the life of Creighton is very like that of Stubbs. After a time of teaching in Oxford they were both presented to country livings in the Church of England; later both held chairs of history, Stubbs at Oxford and Creighton at Cambridge; and both finally were made bishops. It is doubtless wise to select men of learning to fill these important positions, but the administrative duties of a large diocese leave little margin for the private work of students. Creighton's claim to fame must rest upon the work accomplished before he became Bishop first of Peterborough and afterwards of London. His largest book, *The History of the Papacy*, is dry and hard reading. Lord Acton spoke of this work, when the first two volumes appeared, as being marked by a fulness and accuracy which were "prodigious in volumes which are but the prelude to an introduction, and have been composed in the intervals of severer duty"; but Acton thought poorly of the third and fourth volumes. It is strange that such a man as Creighton—a brilliant, incisive talker, epigrammatic and picturesque—failed to make his books brighter than they are.

Perhaps the characteristics of this Oxford school of history are best combined in Samuel Rawson Gardiner. Although he had no private income Gardiner set himself to perform the unremunerative task of writing a history of England during the period between 1603 and 1660. The work occupied him for forty years; and the time which was not devoted to this task had to be spent in lecturing, examining, or writing text books, in order to make sufficient money to live. His life was singularly lonely. He stood much aloof from his contemporaries, and there is no evidence of intimate intercourse between him and Stubbs, Freeman, Creighton or Green. It is this absence of the personal element which has condemned him to relative obscurity and partially explains why it was not until he was sixty-five that his worth was recognised. He was then, on the death of Froude, offered the regius professorship of history at Oxford. He declined the honour, because he felt that its duties might interfere with the task he had set himself to do. In spite of this devotion he did not complete his history, in fact he did not even reach the death of Cromwell. What makes the work of Gardiner of value is its extreme fairness, and its freedom from all personal bias. In this attribute lies also the cause of its want of popularity. It has no striking features, nor any lively narratives.

§ 7. *The Philosophical Historians*

Perhaps what we miss most in these modern historians of the last section is an interest in philosophy. On this side the group of Oxford men were deficient. There was however another historian, a contemporary and a member of the same university but not of the same school, in whom it was conspicuously strong. This was Charles Henry Pearson (1830—1894), who won fame at the end of his life by the remarkable volume entitled *National Life and Character.* His *Early and Middle Ages of England,* though scholarly and able, had only provoked a venomous attack by Freeman. *National Life and Character* is not a history, but rather an essay in political philosophy, brilliant, but excessively discursive. The mournful conclusion at which Pearson arrives is that the day is drawing near when the lower races will predominate over the higher, and when the higher will lose their noblest attributes.

The element of philosophy is prominent also in John Robert Seeley (1834—1895), and its prominence is the cause of the opposition to him which may be detected in Creighton, who found him professor of modern history in Cambridge when he himself went there as professor of ecclesiastical history. Seeley was the son of the author of *The Greatest of all the Plantagenets*, a historian of considerable eminence; but it was not by following in the lines of his father's greatness that the son first won fame. He began life as a classical lecturer in Trinity College, Cambridge, whence he passed as professor of Latin to University College, London, in succession to F. W. Newman, the author of a famous heretical book, *Phases of Faith*, and brother of Cardinal Newman. It may be that there is spiritual as well as bodily contagion in environment; it is at least curious to notice that Seeley too, from this London chair of Latin, disturbed the orthodox world by *Ecce Homo*, a book which puzzled it and won for its author a popularity he never gained by his still more powerful work as historian.

Seeley's books fall into two divisions, theological and historical. To the former class belong *Ecce Homo* and *Natural Religion*. Both were enigmas to their readers, who could not make out what manner of man their anonymous author was, nor why he had written upon religion. He seemed to stand half-way between the believer and the doubter. In *Ecce Homo* he tries to build up the character of Christ as man. In the preface he speaks of "Christ as the creator of modern theology and religion," and in the end of the book he declares that "the achievement of Christ, in founding by his single will and power a structure so durable and so universal, is like no other achievement which history records." *Natural Religion* was promised as a sequel to *Ecce Homo*; but the author had travelled far in the sixteen years which intervened between the two books, and in the latter we seem to see rather the student of Goethe than the disciple of Christ.

Seeley's historical works are marked by a similar predilection for ideas as distinguished from mere narrative. *The Expansion of England* deals with the policy of England in the eighteenth century, calling special attention to the marvellous growth of the British Empire and to the vital importance of that growth as a fact in the history of the world. *The Growth of British Policy* is closely allied to it, but takes a wider and completer view of foreign policy from the accession of Elizabeth to the union of the parliaments of England and Scotland. Seeley dwells here upon the pride and confidence in England which sprang from the defeat of Spain; and that pride and confidence are the inspiration of his work. He was one of the earliest and ablest of the writers who swept away the idea, prevalent in the middle of the nineteenth century, that colonies were a burden and a danger, and who advocated the federation of the British Empire. Seeley's longest and most learned book, but also his least satisfactory one, was his *Life and Times of Stein.* Its theme is the remaking of Prussia and her rise against Napoleon. It is not a biography but rather a history of the time of Stein.

Perhaps the best method to adopt in order to understand Seeley's writings is to seek for his own conception of the universe. To his mind the State was not a collection of statesmen, or a roll of citizens, or a mechanical system of wheels and pinions, but a great organic reality, the inspiration of the higher life, something which could be *felt*, but could by no means be reduced to logical formulae. "Who," he says, "can describe that which unites men?" This lofty conception animated his lectures and thrilled his pupils, and sent warm living blood coursing through his writings. It inspired his theological as well as his historical writings. It is the keynote of his central chapter on the "enthusiasm of humanity" in *Ecce Homo*; and in *Natural Religion* it causes him to dwell on the power of religion to elevate the life of man as a social being.

William Edward Hartpole Lecky (1838—1903) had much in common with Seeley. The first historical work of both was marked by the philosophic spirit. Lecky's *History of the Rise and Influence of the Spirit of Rationalism in Europe* was an astonishing book, considering that it was written by a young man of twenty-seven. The world asked by what magic he had been able to crowd into so few years so much reading. There had been no one to show him the way. He had been educated at Trinity College, Dublin, and had taken his degree there; but the learning of his *Rationalism in Europe* lay far out of the beaten track of colleges and universities. He had gathered it for himself from the bookshelves of the Italian libraries; and what he wrote has the attraction of new material presented by a fresh mind. Everything interested him, and all sorts of curious details about witchcraft, trial by fire and water, and other customs of a half-civilised period are given in his work. They are recorded, not for their own sake, but to illustrate the nature and development of the human intellect. A similar spirit animates *The History of European Morals from Augustus to Charlemagne.* There is no narrative of events, but instead the aim of the writer is to extract from the period reviewed the moral conceptions which prevailed in it. It was a great task, and on the whole it was successfully accomplished. Lecky's chief defect was lack of imagination: he could not live in the past and judge its shortcomings by the standard of the time. For this reason his tendency is to be unsympathetic, and in his treatment of monasticism he is distinctly harsh. His longest work, the *History of England in the Eighteenth Century*, is however singularly fair-minded and impartial.

Much of it deals with the affairs of Ireland; and whether he writes of the relations of England and Ireland, or of the strife between Protestants and Catholics, Lecky succeeds in holding the balance fairly. Though he was a patriotic Irishman, his patriotism is sane and sensible, and there is no distortion of facts.

In later years Lecky reverted to his early philosophic tendency in the choice of subjects. *Democracy and Liberty* and the weaker *Map of Life* appeared in the nineties. In the former he indicates his belief that the special danger of democracy is that of undue interference with individual liberty. He objects to tyranny in the shape of trade unions, as well as in the shape of a monarch or an aristocracy.

Contemporary with Lecky was another historian who took all historical knowledge as his province, choosing for his special theme the wide subject of liberty. John Dalberg Acton, Lord Acton (1834—1902), was professor of history at Cambridge and probably the most learned teacher of his subject in Europe. Unfortunately most of his store of learning is buried in his grave. The history of liberty which he planned was left unfinished, and the volume of lectures, the letters of Quirinus on the Ecumenical Council and some scattered articles, are a poor remainder from so great a man.

Frederic William Maitland (1850—1906), who held a professorship in law, not history, far surpasses his contemporary Acton in the importance of his writings. It is fairly safe to say that no English scholar of the last half-century is more likely than Maitland to stand higher in reputation in the year 2000 than he does at the present time. Maitland has written for the most part on highly technical subjects, and is in consequence comparatively little read. But the few experts who are best entitled to an opinion have pronounced decisively in his favour.

Further, he was not only a profound student of history, but a most skilful writer; and they who read him, undeterred by technicality of subject, usually find him not only intelligible but interesting. Finally, by his *Roman Canon Law in England* Maitland has overthrown a theory of Church history and swept away a whole library written in support of it. Such an achievement can be set to the credit of few historians; and, as our estimate of their importance must depend in a large measure on what they have accomplished, it is evident that Maitland's reputation must rise in proportion as the importance of this phase of his work is realised.

It is strange that of all the historians who have been mentioned Carlyle alone devoted an important work to the greatest event of the recent past—the French Revolution. Sir Archibald Alison tried to supply the want with a laborious *History of Europe during the French Revolution*, an abridged edition of which took its place among the school books of the forties, because it was the best account of an event in which people were profoundly interested. This singular deficiency was not due to want of interest in the movement; perhaps it was owing to the very greatness and wide scope of the subject.

§ 8. *Military History*

The military aspect of the story of the French Revolution proved less embarrassing than the political, and in his *History of the War in the Peninsula* Sir William Napier (1785—1860) produced one of the best narratives of military operations in the language. Napier was a soldier and the descendant of a line of soldiers. He was the brother of the great Sir Charles Napier, the story of whose campaigns he tells in his *Conquest of Scinde*. He knew the Peninsula as he knew his own land, he had fought in it and he understood the difficulties of those who had to do so. He was familiar with the character of the people. He had access to many papers on the French as well as on the English side; and, though he could see "no good act done by a Spanish junta or a Tory minister," his history is likely to remain the great classical account of the famous contest.

In the same way Alexander William Kinglake (1809—1891) will hold his place with *The Invasion of the Crimea.* Kinglake was not, like Napier, a soldier by profession; but his love of adventure carried him across the Black Sea with the troopships. At that time he was already a practised writer. His *Eöthen,* a description of travels in the East, had caught the public fancy by the charm of its language and the truthful simplicity of the description of scenes which are familiar by name to everyone. Kinglake brought his power of animated description to bear on the battlefields of the Crimea. His chief fault is diffuseness. He took four hundred pages to describe the battle of Inkerman, while Napier told the story of Albuera in eight. But this copiousness is not without its advantages. The condensed style of Napier, though greater than the verbose one of Kinglake, does not find room to give the brave deeds of the individual soldier, which we find in the more lengthy narrative. When Gladstone pronounced Kinglake's book "too bad to live," he was thinking of the political side, on which he declared that, as to the matter within his cognisance, it was entirely void of resemblance to the truth; when he added that it was "too good to die," he was doubtless thinking of its vivacity and eminent readableness.

The only other work in this department of history which may fitly be put in line with the great histories of Napier and Kinglake is G. F. R. Henderson's (1854—1903) *Stonewall Jackson and the Civil War,* an admirable biography and a masterly study of that part of the great American Civil War in which Jackson figured. Few biographers are more human, and probably no descriptions of campaigns are at once more satisfying to the professional reader and more clear to the layman. There has scarcely in recent years been a better example of a great theme treated in a great manner.

§ 2. *Students of the Origins.*

Sharon Turner, 1768—1847.
History of the Anglo-Saxons, 1799—1805.
J. M. Kemble, 1807—1857.
The Saxons in England, 1849.
Francis Palgrave, 1788—1861.
History of Normandy and of England, 1851—1864.
Richard Chenevix Trench, 1807—1886.
On the Study of Words, 1851.
English Past and Present, 1855.
Friedrich Max Müller, 1823—1900.
Languages of the Seat of War in the East, 1855.
The Science of Language, 1861—1863.
Chips from a German Workshop, 1867—1875.

§ 3. *Ancient History.*

Sir George Cornewall Lewis, 1806—1863.
Inquiry on the Credibility of Early Roman History, 1855.
Thomas Arnold, 1795—1842.
History of Rome, 1838—1843.
Connop Thirlwall, 1797—1875.
History of Greece, 1835—1844.
George Grote, 1794—1871.
History of Greece, 1846—1856.
George Finlay, 1799—1875.
History of Greece from its Conquest by the Romans, 1844—1861.
Henry Hart Milman, 1791—1868.
History of the Jews, 1830.
History of Christianity under the Empire, 1840.
History of Latin Christianity, 1850—1855.

§ 4. *Hallam and Macaulay.*

Henry Hallam, 1777—1859.
  The State of Europe during the Middle Ages, 1818.
  The Constitutional History of England, 1827.
  An Introduction to the Literature of Europe, 1837—1839.
Thomas Babington Macaulay, 1800—1859.
  Critical and Historical Essays, 1843.
  History of England, 1848—1861.

§ 5. *Froude.*

James Anthony Froude, 1818—1894.
  The Nemesis of Faith, 1849.
  History of England, 1856—1870.
  Short Studies on Great Subjects, 1867—1883.
  The English in Ireland, 1872—1874.
  Thomas Carlyle, 1882—1884.
  Oceana, 1886.

§ 6. *The Oxford Group.*

Edward Augustus Freeman, 1823—1892.
  History of the Norman Conquest, 1867—1879.
  The Reign of William Rufus, 1882.
  The History of Sicily, 1891—1894.
William Stubbs, 1825—1901.
  The Constitutional History of England, 1873—1878.
  The Early Plantagenets, 1874.
John Richard Green, 1837—1883.
  A Short History of the English People, 1874.
  A History of the English People, 1877—1880.
  The Making of England, 1881.
Mandell Creighton, 1843—1901.
  Simon de Montfort, 1876.
  History of the Papacy, 1882—1894.
Samuel Rawson Gardiner, 1829—1902.
  History of England from the Accession of James I, 1863—1901.

§ 7. *The Philosophical Historians.*

Charles Henry Pearson, 1830—1894.
The Early and Middle Ages of England, 1861.
National Life and Character, 1893.
John Robert Seeley, 1834—1895.
Ecce Homo, 1865.
The Life and Times of Stein, 1878.
Natural Religion, 1882.
The Expansion of England, 1883.
The Growth of British Policy, 1895.
W. E. H. Lecky, 1838—1903.
The Rise and Influence of the Spirit of Rationalism in Europe, 1865.
History of European Morals, 1869.
History of England in the Eighteenth Century, 1878—1890.
Democracy and Liberty, 1896.
John Dalberg Acton, Lord Acton, 1834—1902.
Frederic William Maitland, 1850—1906.
The History of English Law before Edward I (with Sir F. Pollock), 1895.
Domesday Book and Beyond, 1897.
Township and Borough, 1898.
Roman Canon Law in England, 1898.
Archibald Alison, 1792—1867.
History of Europe during the French Revolution, 1833—1842.

§ 8. *Military History.*

W. F. P. Napier, 1785—1860.
History of the War in the Peninsula, 1828—1840.
Alexander William Kinglake, 1809—1891.
Eöthen, 1844.
The Invasion of the Crimea, 1863—1887.
G. F. R. Henderson, 1854—1903.
Stonewall Jackson and the Civil War, 1898.

CHAPTER V

BIOGRAPHY AND CRITICISM

§ 1. *The Biographers*

THE writing of biography is, both in England and elsewhere, a thing of late development. In the earlier periods we find stray books of the kind, and in the latter part of the eighteenth century we meet with the conspicuous examples of Johnson's *Lives of the Poets*, and Boswell's great *Life* of Johnson himself. But the recognised *business* of biography hardly begins until the nineteenth century.

Among the biographical works of the Victorian era, Lockhart's *Life of Scott* holds the highest place. The author had already tried his hand at the difficult task of writing a *Life of Burns*, and accomplished it with such success that Andrew Lang pronounces him to be, of all the poet's biographers, "he who divides us least." But, admirable though this life of Burns is, the *Life of Scott* is much greater. For in this work Lockhart had the advantage of being in perfect harmony with his subject. "Lockhart," says Lang, "had been born to love Scott, and beyond even that regard which Scott's works awaken in every gentle heart, to make him by all men yet more beloved." Lockhart was brought up in Edinburgh, his national and his professional interests were the same as Scott's, he moved in the same circle, and he made the connexion closer by becoming Scott's son-in-law. In spite of this intimate relationship and profound love, he was able to retain his clearness of vision and sanity of judgment. He saw the greatness of Scott, but he also saw his weakness, and knew how to deal with it without falling into excess, as Macaulay and Taine do when they touch upon the love of Scott for wealth. Lockhart makes it clear that Scott's love of money was intimately connected with the higher dreams of his imagination. He aspired to be the founder of a family, and Abbotsford, his house, was "a romance in stone and lime." The almost unbounded hospitality exercised there for years was a realisation of the visions which constantly filled his mind. His ambition needed more money than he could afford, and was therefore a mistaken one, but it was far from vulgar.

Perhaps the most trying test to apply to a biographer is his use of ordinary everyday incidents, so as to reveal the character of his subject, and to give life to the picture. Lockhart has done this task with masterly skill. He has gathered innumerable details of the life of Scott. There are stories of the hunting parties, the joyous picnics, the slow drives through Edinburgh, where every stone had for Scott a memory, of the famous visitors who came and went, of the faithful servants who never went, of the beloved dogs whose one fault was that they could not live for ever. Lockhart brings all into his picture. And in the centre is the "shirra," as Scott liked to be called, the soul of everything, his big heart overflowing with affection and his humour giving zest to every hour of the day.

Even if there were no Boswell's *Life of Johnson*, this admirable biography would suffice to refute the notion that the lives of literary men are too uneventful to be suitable for biography. No judgment could be more mistaken. Nearly all the finest biographies of the world have men of letters for their subject. Great explorers are but dimly seen through their wanderings, great soldiers are usually silent, and great statesmen have their lips sealed by considerations of policy. The literary man, on the other hand, is usually a good talker, a ready letter writer and an outspoken critic; and in all these ways he is piling up material for his biographer.

Of the lives of the literary men of this period, except Carlyle's *Life of Sterling* and Froude's *Carlyle*, there is none to compare with Lockhart's *Life of Scott*. Perhaps the least distant is Stanley's *Life of Arnold*. The task of writing about Arnold was congenial to Stanley, and his life of the great headmaster is the best work he did. Arnold was a man of high character with the great gift of knowing his own mind. It simply remained for his biographer to follow his lead; and that, for Stanley, was easy. The pupil had been made upon the model of his beloved master and saw eye to eye with him in most things. Even the vexed question whether Arnold, with his heterodox views, had still a legitimate place in the Church of England, presented no difficulty to the man who did not see why Roman Catholics should not be members of the Church of England, if it were only made legal.

The Life of Goethe by George Henry Lewes was a task of much greater difficulty than that undertaken by Stanley. But Lewes did it so thoroughly that his book remained until recently an authority even in Germany itself. The biographer-in-ordinary of the period was however John Forster (1812—1876). He wrote the lives of many statesmen and men of letters, and is memorable chiefly for two, *The Life of Landor* and *The Life of Dickens*, because in these cases he is an original authority. For Dickens especially Forster must always remain the principal source of information. He was the close friend of Dickens, who seems to have put his very soul into Forster's keeping.

This close connexion set Forster a hard task, and brought upon him the charge of writing the story of this intimate friendship rather than the biography of the great novelist.

The Life of Milton by David Masson (1822—1907) is widely different from *The Life of Dickens*, being more historical than biographical. When a man attempts to write the "life and times," he necessarily sacrifices something of true biography, which is almost independent of "times." But there remain two biographies which are deserving of brief notice because of their close connexion with the literary history of the time. These are Samuel Smiles's *Memoir of John Murray* and Margaret Oliphant's *William Blackwood and his Sons.* They deal with the two houses which, of all the publishing houses in England, have had most of the literary spirit. Though Byron was the author of the sneer, "Now Barabbas was a publisher," his own relations with the founder of the house of Murray prove that he had no very serious meaning in uttering it; and though Scott, in anger, once sent a message to the first William Blackwood, to say that he was "one of the Black Hussars of Literature, who neither give nor receive criticism," no one knew better than he the solid worth of the founder of the Edinburgh firm. For the literary history of the first half of the nineteenth century these two books are treasures of great value.

§ 2. *The Edinburgh Critics*

When in 1802 Francis Jeffrey, Sydney Smith, Henry Brougham and Francis Horner met in Edinburgh to found a critical journal, they were conscious that they were taking a new departure; but they hardly realised its far-reaching importance. Their periodical *The Edinburgh Review* was to them something of a joke. Under the cover of anonymity they could air their wit at the expense of their neighbours, and pronounce sentence upon newcomers, safe from detection under the editorial "we." The *Review* grew to be a force in the country its promoters had little dreamed of. They were Whigs, and though they had not meant to be the organ of their party, they became so. Therefore strong Tories like Scott felt bound to start *The Quarterly Review* as a medium for their Toryism. The first number of the *Quarterly* appeared in 1808. A few years later, in 1817, *Blackwood's Magazine* took the field. It came out more frequently and was written in a lighter tone than the two quarterlies. These periodicals were followed in 1820 by *The London Magazine*, in 1824 by the serious *Westminster Review* and in 1830 by the bright and witty *Fraser's Magazine*. In 1827 *The Athenæum* and in 1828 the *Spectator* appeared. The five last were published in London, but in the beginning of periodical literature the seat of government was undoubtedly in the capital of the north.

Edinburgh had inherited a tradition of literature and learning. In it Allan Ramsay and Ferguson, Hume, Robertson, Adam Smith and Dugald Stewart had all lived and worked. Their young successors had the genius of Scott to draw them out. They felt they were expected to live up to the traditions of their city, and they did so. The setting up in their midst of two of the three most important of British publishing firms—Constable, who was connected with Scott's novels, and William Blackwood—ensured a market for the wares of literary adventurers; and the appearance of the band of verse writers who are grouped together under the shadow of Wordsworth, and known as the Lake Poets, supplied the budding critics with a target for their wit. There was neither doubt nor diffidence in this group of literary free-lances. Brought up upon the laws of verse practised by Pope, they condemned the work of Wordsworth. Jeffrey began his review of *The Excursion* with the words, "This will never do." Southey, who was critic as well as poet, met Jeffrey with the retort: "*He* crush *The Excursion*! Tell him he might as well fancy he could crush Skiddaw." At a later date, in *Blackwood's Magazine*, Lockhart wrote objectionable articles on *The Cockney School of Poetry*; and Wilson, another of this northern group, though he had previously praised Wordsworth with generous warmth, called *The Excursion* "the worst poem of any character in the language." But while these ardent young Scots were vainly assailing Skiddaw and blindly misplacing their youthful enthusiasm, Coleridge and Hazlitt in the south had with open arms bid the recent writers of the romantic school welcome. The Edinburgh critics were a people sitting in darkness, and they failed to recognise the light that had broken through. For the *Edinburgh* reviewers Pope had pronounced the last word, and no progress seemed possible beyond his *Essay on Man*, *The Dunciad* and *Satires and Epistles*. So it will always be; to the end there will be some who will fight with all their strength for the old methods against the new.

Most of the Edinburgh critics whom we have mentioned belong to the revolutionary period rather than to the Victorian era; but Lockhart and Wilson are two who come into our time. John Wilson (1785—1854) was the senior of the two. He was the son of a Paisley manufacturer, and, going to Magdalen College, Oxford, he won there a high reputation for talent, and a still higher for athletics. As the loss of the fortune he had inherited from his father made it necessary for him to qualify himself for some lucrative profession, he turned to the bar. But he only received one brief, and with that he knew not what to do. He found his real work, as well as his best chance of winning a livelihood, in the pages of *Blackwood's Magazine*. Here, under the name of Christopher North, he wrote the famous papers known as the *Noctes Ambrosianae* and *The Recreations of Christopher North*.

John Gibson Lockhart (1794—1854) we already know as the biographer and also the son-in-law of Sir Walter Scott. He likewise worked with Wilson upon the staff of "Maga," the tender name for *Blackwood's Magazine*; but after his marriage with Sophia Scott he was drawn into the Abbotsford circle and his connexion with the *Blackwood* reviewers became less close. In 1825 he accepted the editorship of *The Quarterly Review* and moved to London, where he remained in this office for twenty-eight years. He resigned the editorship a few months before his lonely death. He had outlived not only Scott but all Scott's children, most of his contemporaries and all but one of his own family. A conservative critic, he hardly liked or encouraged new poets with new ways. He rode roughshod over the verses of the young Tennyson, as he had depreciated Keats, with the rest of what he called the Cockney school. Still, to be just to him, under his editorship of the *Quarterly*, if not from his pen, a considerable number of the younger poets received favourable treatment. Among those who are appreciated we find Fanny Kemble, the erratic Hartley Coleridge, Henry Taylor, John Sterling, Aubrey de Vere, Elizabeth Barrett Browning, Mrs Norton and a group of other poetesses. The articles on Taylor and Fanny Kemble were by Lockhart.

§ 3. *Leigh Hunt and De Quincey*

It is a mistake to suppose that the early Victorian era was particularly strong in criticism. Hazlitt, Coleridge and Lamb were dead. Of the younger men the only one of first-rate importance who was writing criticism was Carlyle; for Macaulay's essays were, as he himself said, historical far more than critical. In point of fact, much of the best criticism of that time was the work of two survivors of the previous age—Leigh Hunt and De Quincey.

James Henry Leigh Hunt (1784—1859) put his best

work into *Examiners*, *Tatlers*, *Reflectors*, *Indicators*, etc., etc., which he edited in order to make a living. He found it a hard task to make both ends meet, and Mrs Carlyle, who lived near him in Cheyne Row, becomes wrathful over the frequent borrowings by her neighbours, the penniless Hunts. The hard-working father had an astonishing fertility of mind. He practically wrote the four pages of the daily *Tatler* himself. As a critic he was remarkably open-minded. To him belongs the honour of being able to see the enchantment in Keats while *Blackwood* was scoffing at him. Yet, like almost all his contemporaries, he is strangely inconsistent with himself.

Hunt's contemporary Thomas de Quincey (1785—1859) made the acquaintance of Wilson at the Lakes, and was by him introduced to Blackwood, who found him at once a delight and a worry. De Quincey never could be ready in time; but he was invaluable as a contributor, for he was familiar with many subjects, and able to theorise even where he had but scanty knowledge. He wrote exquisite English. His weakness was that the music of his own phrases tempted him to use words out of proportion to the meaning. In criticism, when De Quincey is at his best he is unsurpassed. The famous essay *On the Knocking at the Gate in Macbeth* is perhaps the finest example in English of the power of imagination to throw light upon a dark passage. But in criticism as in other things the greater part of his work is marred by diffuseness.

§ 4. *Matthew Arnold*

Before Hunt and De Quincey died in 1859, a considerable number of notable critics of a younger generation had made their appearance. Several of them were great in other things besides criticism. Ruskin, Thackeray, Dante Rossetti and Matthew Arnold were all workers in divers fields of literature as well as critics. Three of them may be briefly dismissed, as far as their critical writings are concerned; yet no account of the criticism of the period should wholly pass them over. Thackeray's *English Humourists* is, even for those who differ most widely from him on special points, or with regard to particular writers, among the most valuable of the books which deal with the eighteenth century. Dante Rossetti need only be named for the sake of his *Hand and Soul*, the best extant statement of the principles of the Pre-Raphaelite school. And the *Modern Painters* of Ruskin, the first volume of which appeared in 1843, contains a body of literary criticism second in importance only to the criticism of painting, which is the professed theme of that very discursive and varied work.

Matthew Arnold is different. His critical work is of an importance which rivals, and even, in the opinion of many, surpasses that of his poetry. Criticism was, in Arnold's case, a later development than the pursuit of poetry. His first volume of poems was published in 1849; his first piece of memorable criticism was the essay prefixed to another volume of poems four years later. But we have seen that within twenty years of his first appearance he had almost ceased to write poetry, while he remained a critic to the end of his life.

Arnold defines criticism as "the endeavour, in all branches of knowledge, theology, philosophy, history, art, science, to see the object as in itself it really is." He meant therefore a great deal more than the criticism of books. He felt that England had fallen behind other nations in this art, and as his highest desire was to be of use to England he tried to give her what she had not. Arnold thought that the English critics had gone astray in their great admiration of romanticism. He himself was fully conscious of its defects. He never enthusiastically loved Shelley, and only late in life found the full charm of Keats. Coleridge irritated him as often as he pleased him. He admired the spirit and power of Elizabethan literature, but found it "steeped in humours and whimsicality up to its very lips"; and though no one has praised Shakespeare more nobly than he in his well-known sonnet, he insisted that Milton was a safer model for England. He urged that the revolt against the laws that guided the eighteenth century had gone too far, and that the liberty which that revolt had won for England was in danger of degenerating into licence. Arnold was by nature unsympathetic towards romance, partly because he felt its apparent lawlessness. To him England was "the native home of intellectual eccentricity of all kinds," and he wanted to set this right. He thought he saw one means of doing so by turning our interest to French literature rather than to German. He did not set the genius of France above that of Germany. The line, "France, famed in all arts, in none supreme," expresses his deliberate judgment. He held that she had no genius fit to measure against Goethe, to say nothing of Shakespeare. But he thought we had already too many of the characteristics of the Teutonic race. What he saw in French literature was the definiteness of meaning, clearness of expression, open-mindedness, elasticity and brightness of intelligence which we needed. By quoting from his essay *On the Function of Criticism at the Present Time*, we can get at his ideals. He sums up the rule for English criticism in the word *disinterestedness*, and explains that he means "keeping aloof from what is called the practical view of things. To try and approach truth from one side after another, not to strive or cry, nor to persist in pressing forward, on any one side, with violence and self will,—it is only thus, it seems to me, that mortals may hope to gain any vision of the mysterious Goddess, whom we shall never see except in outline, but only thus even in outline."

Along with this disinterestedness Arnold insists that the critic must have knowledge of the best that has been thought and said in the world ; and in this way, by seeing how other nations do what we are doing, we shall avoid narrow mindedness. But although he saw the need of knowledge, Arnold was fully alive to the dangers of a vast load of learning. What it was vital to know was not *everything* that had been thought and said, but the *best*.

Besides the volumes which criticise literature Arnold has three other groups of critical writings which deserve mention. As assistant-commissioner under an educational commission appointed by Government to enquire into the state of popular education, it was his duty to report upon the schools and universities of France and Germany. Then we have belonging to the second group his political criticisms, such as the pamphlet *England and the Italian Question* and *Culture and Anarchy*, which is described as "an essay in political and social criticism." But his finest criticism on the social side is contained in *Friendship's Garland*. These delightful essays in the form of letters are the richest of all Arnold's writings in wit and humour. Yet he was most unwilling to reprint them. In the third group we have his theological criticisms—*St Paul and Protestantism*, *Literature and Dogma*, *God and the Bible* and *Last Essays on Church and Religion*. These books are called for convenience theological ; but they are really the layman's protest against the commonly accepted idea that only a trained student of divinity can pronounce judgment upon the truths of religion. Arnold urges the man of science, the philosopher, the students of literature and history—all seekers after truth—to believe that they too have the opportunity of seeing phases of the truth and the right to express their views.

§ 5. *Brown, Stephen, Henley*

No other critic of the time equalled Arnold in importance and influence, but Walter Bagehot, whom we have discussed amongst the philosophers, may be mentioned in passing for the sake of his excellent literary essays, and Dr John Brown (1810—1882) for the exquisite delicacy of his taste, and also because no other equally convenient opportunity can be found for mentioning the author of *Rab and his Friends*. Brown knew Edinburgh in the days of its literary greatness. Jeffrey had congratulated him on his *Locke and Sydenham*; he had with loving reverence watched Sir Walter Scott limp along Princes Street. He has left too few reminiscences of those days, but he has given us the touching stories of little *Marjorie Fleming*, *Rab and his Friends* and *Our Dogs*. Each is perfect in its way, and by them his fame will live. The story of Rab is very simple and very short. A big dog, his hard worked friend the carrier and the carrier's sick wife are the subjects; but none of them can be forgotten. No one ever wrote better than Dr John Brown upon dogs, and few can surpass him in criticism, where success depends upon sympathy and fineness of feeling and a delicate sense of the poetical. It is these qualities that give value to the paper on the death of Thackeray, to that on Henry Vaughan, and above all to the faultless criticism of the old Scotch song, "Oh, I'm wat, wat."

It will suffice in this section to notice two more of the critics who were for different reasons prominent in the later years of the nineteenth century. One of these is Leslie Stephen (1832—1904), who married a daughter of Thackeray. He edited the early volumes of the *Dictionary of National Biography*, and did a surprising amount of work besides criticism. Indeed his most solid performances were more philosophical than critical. He was a rationalist, and a close student of the English thinkers of the eighteenth century and of the Utilitarian school. And these tendencies in his mind supply the key to his criticisms. Stephen was eminently sound and solid, without being heavy. He was somewhat cold in his atmosphere, distrusting impressionism and shunning appreciations and enthusiasm. He brought back into criticism not a little of the spirit of the eighteenth century, for he agreed with Arnold that the reaction against it had been pushed too far by the romanticists. He was at his best in a sort of condensed biography, rather than in strictly literary criticism. Examples of this special gift may be found in his *Studies of a Biographer* and in his various contributions to the series of *English Men of Letters*.

The other literary critic referred to is William Ernest Henley (1849—1903), whose virile energy is impressed upon his prose essays as well as upon his poems. No man of the younger generation exercised greater influence over his contemporaries, none was more fearless and independent in judgment. His faults are excessive dogmatism and a tendency to crude denunciation. His merit is an extraordinary power of penetrating to the heart of the matter. His brilliant essay on Burns would not easily be surpassed were it not so hard and unsympathetic.

§ 6. *The Criticism of Art*

The criticism of art, as distinct from literature, is, in England, a special feature of the nineteenth century. There had been, indeed, at an earlier date, a few attempts such as the *Discourses* of Sir Joshua Reynolds; but before the nineteenth century nothing like a literature on the subject existed. Already however in the early decades of that century we see the beginnings of such a literature.

Lamb and Hazlitt both wrote on the subject, and the latter's *Conversations of Northcote* was warmly praised by Ruskin. To those early years belong in substance, though not in date of publication, the fascinating *Autobiography* of the painter Benjamin Haydon, one of the most remarkable books of self-revelation ever penned. But all these earlier writings seem fragmentary and amateurish in comparison with the aesthetic work of John Ruskin (1819—1900). He was the son of a wine merchant who was descended from a line of Scottish lairds. His parents were cousins and he was their only child. He never went to school, but he had within his own home, till he went to Oxford, influences well fitted to develop his nature. His father was a man singularly sensitive to the best in literature and art. In *Praeterita* Ruskin describes him as "an absolutely beautiful reader of the best poetry and prose." He read aloud to his boy "all the Shakespeare comedies and historical plays again and again, all Scott and all Don Quixote." Thus Ruskin under his father's guidance read the right books. With him he also saw the right things. In the summer the family would combine business with pleasure, and visit, in search of orders for wine, the old halls and castles of England. In 1833 Prout's *Sketches in Flanders and Germany* sent them on a tour up the Rhine and into Switzerland. The gift of an illustrated edition of *Italy* by Rogers was one of the most memorable incidents of Ruskin's youth; for in it he met for the first time with the work of Turner, whom he was destined afterwards to bring into his kingdom.

The mother of Ruskin was rigidly evangelical. Both father and son acquiesced in the evangelicalism rather than shared it. Speaking of his father Ruskin says: "Though he went to church with a resigned countenance, I knew very well that he liked going just as little as I did." His mother meant her boy to be an evangelical clergyman, but this plan was frustrated by the stern sabbatarianism of an aunt, his father's sister, who gave him cold mutton for Sunday's dinner, "which—as I much preferred it hot—greatly diminished the influence of *The Pilgrim's Progress*." His mother was almost as uncompromising as his aunt about the keeping of Sunday, and when the father and son on their foreign tours indulged in walks on Sunday, they did so "with unholy joy, dashed with a sense that they were children of perdition." It was not until he was verging on forty that Ruskin went so far as to draw on Sunday, "with a dimly alarmed sense of its being a new fact in existence" for him. There is no doubt that he owed much to his mother for the unceasing care with which she taught him to know his Bible. The mother and son began with the opening of Genesis and read steadily through, day by day, omitting nothing, till they reached the end of the Apocalypse; when they began over again. The result was that, from this intimate knowledge of the Scriptures, Ruskin acquired a backbone to his thought and style, which otherwise might have been deficient in force.

As has already been said, his moth reexpected him to become a minister; and his father looked to see him a poet, like Byron, only pious, and a preacher, like Bossuet, only Protestant. The parents' forecast of the destiny of their gifted child was not far astray; for his work was to preach in poetic prose, though not from the pulpit. As critic of painting and architecture it was his mission to preach the religion of beauty, and then later, as a socialist and reformer, the religion of humanity. He was a preacher from his cradle. There was always in him the habit of mind which finds in nature a text for sermons. "Mountains," he says, "mould character and implant religion; and indeed this is true of nature in all her forms. Supposing all circumstances otherwise the same with respect to two individuals, the one who loves nature most will be *always* found to have more *faith in God* than the other." But it is necessary here to point out that consistency is a virtue for which we must not look in Ruskin. Elsewhere he tells us, in direct opposition, that "the intense love of nature is, in modern times, characteristic of persons not of the first order of intellect, but of brilliant imagination, quick sympathy, and undefined religious principle, suffering also under strong and ill governed passions." A profound sense of the importance of truth to nature lies however at the heart of all his criticisms in art and literature. "The more I think of it," he says, "I find the conclusion more impressed upon me,—that the greatest thing a human soul ever does is to *see* something, and tell what it *saw* in a plain way. Hundreds of people can talk for one who can think, but thousands of people can think for one who can see. To see clearly is poetry, prophecy, and religion,—all in one."

It was this impulse to teach people to *see* which drove him to write *Modern Painters*. The first volume came out when he was twenty-four. He had taken his degree, "a complimentary double fourth," the year before, and had gained the Newdigate prize for his poem *Salsette and Elephanta*. But *Modern Painters* was his first important work. The fresh vigorous criticisms of this unknown "Graduate of Oxford University" and the beauty of the style in which they were expressed showed him to be an artist in words if not with the pencil. He had been stirred to write as he did by the manifest inability of England to appreciate his favourite painter Turner. He had gathered his ideas from the collection of Turner's drawings in the possession of a fellow-enthusiast, a certain Godfrey Windus, a retired coach-builder living at Tottenham. Of him Ruskin writes: "Nobody in all England, at that time,—and Turner was already sixty,—cared, in the true sense of the word, for Turner, but the retired coach-maker of Tottenham, and I."

The success of the first volume of *Modern Painters* settled the course of Ruskin's life. His mother saw that her dream of a son in the church must be given up, and his father sadly laid aside his hope of having a son who would write a *Childe Harold* fit for the Sunday school. They listened with tears to the reading of *Modern Painters*, but the new life it had opened up to their son never wholly satisfied their ambition for him. Their generosity did not cease because of their disappointment. The education of Ruskin by foreign travel and the study of art went on. In 1844 he was in Switzerland, the following year in Italy, a year later again in Switzerland. And it was in that last year that the second volume of *Modern Painters* appeared. Ten years passed before the next two volumes came, and not until 1860 was the fifth and last volume given to the world. It was no wonder that the elder Ruskin felt that he might be dead before the work was ended.

It was neither idleness nor lack of material which caused this delay. The material at the author's command was immense: *Modern Painters* itself is a substantial work for seventeen years of labour. But in addition to it Ruskin had written *The Seven Lamps of Architecture* and *The Stones of Venice*, to say nothing of various other works of less importance.

The publication of the last volume of *Modern Painters* marks the disappearance of Ruskin the art critic, and the emergence of Ruskin the social reformer. Important as is the change, it is an error to suppose that it indicates any inconsistency, or discloses a break in his life. It is only a development. Already in his books upon art it is possible to detect the principles which he afterwards expressed more explicitly and insisted upon more strenuously in those which he devoted to economic and to social questions. There is a passage in *The Seven Lamps* which shows this.

Speaking of the construction of the railways, he complains that we have paid immense sums to men for digging ground from one place and depositing it in another. We have formed a class of men especially reckless, unmanageable and dangerous. We have fostered unwholesome trades. In short, we have forgotten welfare in the pursuit of something miscalled wealth. Now these principles are, in essence, just the principles which Ruskin reiterates in all his economic works, from *Unto this Last* and *Munera Pulveris* to *Fors Clavigera*.

The first named of these three works, which Ruskin always held to contain his finest writing, appeared in the form of essays in *The Cornhill Magazine*, then edited by Thackeray. The ideas were so unpopular that the editor had to stop the series after printing four papers. This adverse criticism made the author keen for battle. "After turning the matter hither and thither in my mind for two years or more," he says, "I resolved to make it the central work of my life to write an exhaustive treatise on Political Economy." Froude, who was then editor of *Fraser's Magazine*, determined, in spite of the experience of Thackeray, to risk publishing Ruskin's new work. So the preface to it was printed in four essays in the years 1862 and 1863. Then the same thing happened again—the public remonstrated, and the articles had to cease. They were collected and published under the title of *Munera Pulveris*, the name selected for the larger work which was never written. *The Crown of Wild Olive*, *Time and Tide* and the series of letters known as *Fors Clavigera* all belong to this economic period, and *Sesame and Lilies* manifests a kindred spirit.

In 1869 Ruskin was chosen to hold the chair of Slade professor of art at Oxford. So great a crowd gathered to hear him that the room in the museum which had been assigned to him could not contain it, and he had to move to the Sheldonian Theatre. Many of his later works were the direct or indirect outcome of this professorship. *Aratra Pentelici*, lectures on sculpture, *The Eagle's Nest*, on the relation between art and science, *Ariadne Florentina*, on engraving on wood and metal, and *Val d'Arno*, on the art of Tuscany, are among the number. The somewhat eccentric enterprise of making a road at Hincksey by the labour of his pupils amused the world. It was a very bad road, but it indicates that Ruskin the economist and social reformer still survived in Ruskin the professor of art.

Ruskin had plenty of absurdities and whimsicalities and inconsistencies; but in spite of them all his permanent value is very great. He discovered Turner, and it was through him that England learned to understand the Venetians. He says with truth that "Tintoret was virtually unseen, Veronese unfelt, Carpaccio not so much as named, when I began to study them." He opened our eyes to the hideousness of the great industrial and mining regions of England; he showed us the sordid ugliness of the modern scramble for wealth, and pointed out how false and mistaken is the modern conception of what really constitutes it.

Ruskin outlived his intellect by many sad years, and the end came slowly in a quiet home amid the Cumberland mountains. He divides men's lives into three great periods—"the days of youth, of labour, and of death. Youth is properly the forming time—that in which a man makes himself, or is made, what he is for ever to be. Then comes the time of labour, when, having become the best he can be, he does the best he can do. Then the time of death, which, in happy lives, is very short: but always a time." This happiness was not his. In his case the "time of death" extended over a greater period than even the seven years he assigned to it in the case of Scott.

During the lifetime of Ruskin, but quite independently

of him, the Pre-Raphaelites were working on lines parallel to his. Thus it would be untrue to say that, had he never lived, his work would have been left entirely undone. These reforming brethren set out to extol and explain the beauties of mediæval art, and also, like Ruskin, to do battle with the false ideals of beauty and worth which had crept into English life. *The Germ* was their magazine, and in it we find the beautifully-written allegorical story of Dante Rossetti called *Hand and Soul*, in which may be found the whole essence of the teaching of the Pre-Raphaelites in art and in poetry. Rossetti holds that the artist's business is to obey the rules he finds written in his own heart. These alone are binding on him. In this sense only was Pre-Raphaelitism a return to nature, for the Pre-Raphaelites were not greatly interested in external nature.

Akin to this school was Walter Pater (1839—1894), whose greatest work, *Marius the Epicurean*, though a short book, was the outcome of six years of concentrated labour. Such laboriousness was characteristic of Pater, and it has left its mark on his fine but frequently over-wrought style. It was his settled conviction (wherein he agreed with Arnold) that the special characteristic of the age was the unmanageable complexity of its interests. Hardly any powers, he thought, were great enough to deal with them, and in consequence he was himself diffident and backward in publication. His own works, which are remarkable for variety of subject, seem to reflect this complexity. But at the core we always find Pater himself. He never can get outside himself, and even the poets and artists whom he criticises have to take his colour. Hence he is most successful in dealing with men of an introspective nature, like himself. He is far less satisfactory in his handling of men like Shakespeare, whose genius is equally at home with the outer world and with the inner. In the case of Pater therefore large allowance must be made for the "personal equation," so that his criticisms are apt to commend themselves rather to a group of admirers than to the world at large. He loved to call them "appreciations," and the word is aptly chosen; they are appreciations rather than judgments.

§ 1. *The Biographers.*

John Gibson Lockhart, 1794—1854.
Life of Burns, 1828.
Life of Scott, 1836—1838.
Arthur Penrhyn Stanley, 1815—1881.
Life of Thomas Arnold, 1844.
George Henry Lewes, 1817—1878.
Life of Goethe, 1855.
John Forster, 1812—1876.
Life and Adventures of Oliver Goldsmith, 1848.
Sir John Eliot, 1864.
Life of Landor, 1869.
Life of Dickens, 1872—1874.
Life of Swift, 1876.
David Masson, 1822—1907.
Life of Milton, 1859—1880.
Samuel Smiles, 1812—1904.
Memoir of John Murray, 1891.
Margaret Oliphant, 1828—1897.
Life of Edward Irving, 1862.
Memoirs of Laurence Oliphant, 1891.
William Blackwood and his Sons, 1897.

§ 2. *The Edinburgh Critics.*

Francis Jeffrey, 1773—1850.
John Wilson, 1785—1854.
Noctes Ambrosianae, 1822—1833.
The Recreations of Christopher North, 1843.

§ 3. *Leigh Hunt and De Quincey.*

Leigh Hunt, 1784—1859.
Imagination and Fancy, 1844.

Wit and Humour, 1846.
Men, Women and Books, 1847.
Autobiography, 1850.

Thomas de Quincey, 1785—1859.
Confessions of an English Opium Eater, 1822.
Autobiographic Sketches, 1853.

§ 4. *Matthew Arnold.*

Matthew Arnold, 1822—1888.
On Translating Homer, 1861.
Essays in Criticism, 1865, 1888.
The Study of Celtic Literature, 1867.
Culture and Anarchy, 1869.
St Paul and Protestantism, 1870.
Friendship's Garland, 1871.
Literature and Dogma, 1873.
God and the Bible, 1875.
Mixed Essays, 1879.
Irish Essays, 1882.
Discourses in America, 1885.

§ 5. *Brown, Stephen, Henley.*

John Brown, 1810—1882.
Horae Subsecivae, 1858—1882.

Leslie Stephen, 1832—1904.
Hours in a Library, 1874—1879.
English Thought in the Eighteenth Century, 1876.
Studies of a Biographer, 1898.
The English Utilitarians, 1900.

William Ernest Henley, 1849—1903.
Views and Reviews, 1890.

§ 6. *The Criticism of Art.*

John Ruskin, 1819—1900.
Modern Painters, 1843—1860.
The Seven Lamps of Architecture, 1849.
The Stones of Venice, 1851—1853.
Pre-Raphaelitism, 1851.
Lectures on Architecture and Painting, 1854.

The Political Economy of Art, 1857.
Unto this Last, (1860)—1862.
Munera Pulveris, (1862—1863)—1872.
Sesame and Lilies, 1865.
The Crown of Wild Olive, 1866.
Time and Tide by Weare and Tyne, 1867.
Lectures on Art, 1870.
Fors Clavigera, 1871—1884.
Praeterita, 1885—1889.
Dante Gabriel Rossetti, 1828—1882.
Hand and Soul, 1850.
Walter Pater, 1839—1894.
Studies in the History of the Renaissance, 1873.
Marius the Epicurean, 1885.
Imaginary Portraits, 1887.
Appreciations, 1889.
Plato and Platonism, 1893
Gaston de Latour, 1896.

CHAPTER VI

THE FRAGMENTS THAT REMAIN

§ 1. *Landor and Minor Writers*

WALTER SAVAGE LANDOR (1775—1864) claims the first place among the miscellaneous writers who remain to be treated. Though he was a man of rare distinction, he was strangely incapable of self-control. The first memorable incident in his history was the outcome of an ungovernable temper: he was sent down from Oxford for an act of violence; and again near the end of his long life he had to leave England in consequence of an action for libel which he had provoked. He married in haste and repented his impulsive action in a leisure of fifty years. He was full of contradictions—a republican yet a haughty aristocrat, a cultured gentleman and a master of English style who dropped his h's, full of love and tenderness yet of ungovernable violence, a classical scholar who carried with him the freakishness of the romantic school. In literature Landor stands alone. His long life stretches like an arch almost across a century. Carlyle, Macaulay, Thackeray, Dickens, the Brontës, George Eliot, Browning, Tennyson and Darwin were all at some time his contemporaries. Dr Johnson was still talking when he was born, and when he died the theory of evolution was shaking the world of science. By reason of his eighty-nine years he takes his place as a writer in Victorian literature, as well as in the literature of the revolutionary period. His earliest poetry was published before the end of the eighteenth century, his latest nearly seventy years after. He wrote poetry all his life, but it is not by his verse that he will be remembered. Three years after his first poetic venture he wrote the poem of *Gebir*, which he sought to make popular by translating it into Latin verse. He delighted in his skill in this decaying art. But what might be expected of a man so eccentric, who believed he could attract readers to an English poem by burying it in a dead language?

Landor's first dramatic work was *Count Julian*, and his last was *The Siege of Ancona*, which came out thirty-four years later. But Landor was no dramatist, and, in his own words, his plays are "no better than imaginary conversations in metre." In his inability to vary his style with the character he is presenting Landor resembles Browning. They are also alike in their inclination to ignore action, and to dwell on a situation just before or just after the crisis in the story.

Landor is greatest in the *Imaginary Conversations*. In these he dealt with matters regarding which his knowledge was ripest and his sympathies keenest, and they contain his greatest achievements in the delineation of character. Long trains of famous persons are passed in review—Socrates, Hannibal, Queen Elizabeth and a score of others, some of ages before the Christian era, others contemporary with the author himself. Landor is happiest among the classical ghosts, where his mastery of dignified English is in harmony with the conversations of the persons he brings back to life. His failures are most conspicuous in his literary criticism, notably in his later dialogue between Southey and Porson on Wordsworth. His earlier view of this poet was so widely different that the reader hesitates to trust the judgment of a man who thus contradicts what he has said before. Of Landor as a critic, Professor Saintsbury writes: "Of judicial quality or qualities, he had not one single trace, and, even putting them out of the question, his intelligence was streaked and flawed by strange veins of positive silliness." Though this judgment requires qualification, and receives it from Professor Saintsbury, it is true that Landor was an unsafe critic. The lawlessness of his character exhibits itself in his condemnations as well as in his panegyrics, but never in his style. His words are chosen for their weight and austerity, and his instinct for expression made him a master of language. He never has been and probably never will be popular. "I shall dine late, but the dining room will be well lighted, the guests few and select," is the well-known expression of his own opinion of the place he will permanently hold in English literature.

Mary Russell Mitford (1786—1855) is another link with the past. We remember her as the little girl who chose a certain number at a lottery office, and in spite of difficulties insisted on having that number and no other. She won the prize, a fortune, which speedily slipped through her father's fingers. She wrote tragedies, but she will live in literature as the author of *Our Village*. Miss Mitford in this book, Mrs Gaskell in *Cranford*, and in America Miss Wilkins in *A Humble Romance* and *A Far-Away Melody*, have given us pictures of rural life which stand supreme in English literature for quiet beauty enlivened by quaint humour. There are no serious situations, just friendly parties, simple love-making, and commonplace interests. Perhaps the sweetest of the pictures of *Our Village* is that of the old maid, her face and body grown grey and aged but her heart still fresh as in her twenties. She finds herself in the company of the lover of those long-gone twenties, and "holds her head," as Miss Mitford says, "on one side with that peculiar air which I have noted in the shyer birds, and ladies in love." The whole is filled with humour and pathos admirably blended.

Though they were younger than Miss Mitford, the two brothers Hare, Julius (1795—1855) and Augustus (1792—1834), are, like her, among those who help to link the Victorian era with the eighteenth century. They were joint authors of *Guesses at Truth*, short essays on all sorts of serious subjects, written in a diffuse manner and expressing pleasantly the thoughts that were in the air at the time. They are now in the back row of the bookshelf, and the fame of the authors rests mainly on the friendship of the younger brother with Sterling and Thirlwall, and on the notice taken by Carlyle of his *Life* of Sterling. Another somewhat commonplace writer was Sir Arthur Helps (1813—1875). Yet Ruskin mentions him with Wordsworth and Carlyle as one of the three moderns to whom he owes most. Helps's *Friends in Council* and *Companions of my Solitude* are collections of essays and dialogues whose merit is common sense and whose vice is the commonplace. William Rathbone Greg (1809—1881) was a man of much superior gifts, yet he never achieved the popularity of Helps. He was one of the Unitarians of Lancashire, a community from which have sprung many men of high ability. He wrote *The Creed of Christendom*, but his best book is *Enigmas of Life*, which went into eighteen editions in twenty years. It deals, like the former book, with problems of ethics and religion.

In the chapter upon poets and poetesses some verses have been quoted from William Brighty Rands which prove his title to a place beside those two great makers of verse for children, Lewis Carroll and R. L. Stevenson. But Rands wrote beautiful and thoughtful prose for men, as well as verse for children. His *Henry Holbeach, Student in Life and Philosophy* is a most remarkable book. Nowhere, not even in the masterly work of George Eliot, is there a descriptive picture which can surpass that of the minister of the Little Meeting—"a shoemaker, self-taught; his heart amply supplied with the milk of human kindness, and his creed blazing with damnation." Yet the world hardly knew the name of the man to whom it owed such literary gems. Rands worked under the pseudonyms of Matthew Browne and Henry Holbeach, and few have thought it worth their while to ask who the unknown writer was.

§ 2. *Travel and Geography*

The nineteenth century ranks so late among the ages that it might be thought there was little room in it for a literature of travel. But although four centuries had passed since the discovery of America, at the beginning of the nineteenth century the far East, the centre of Australia and the heart of Africa were practically unknown to men. Polar exploration was just beginning, and it was the mysterious ending to the arctic voyage of Sir John Franklin which occasioned the expedition of Sir F. L. McClintock. In his *Voyage of the Fox* he narrates the history of his discovery of Franklin's tragic fate. An interest in the ancient history of Egypt was awakened in many by *A Thousand Miles up the Nile*, by Amelia B. Edwards (1831—1892). The rise and fall of the African Nile and the action of its waters upon the crops produced on its banks had from the time of Herodotus given the river a fascination for travellers. Where did the great stream spring from, and what was the cause of its fluctuations? David Livingstone (1813—1873), the famous missionary, was thought to be lost in the central regions of Africa; and this belief gave the enterprising newspaper correspondent Henry Morton Stanley (1841—1904) the opportunity of making himself famous by finding the missing traveller Both threw much light upon the mysteries of the dark continent. But it was John Hanning Speke (1827—1864), an intrepid explorer but a very bad writer, who solved the problem of the great river. The Raleigh of the nineteenth century was Sir Richard Burton (1821—1890). He travelled with Speke, but the two quarrelled violently and parted, and Burton turned to other tasks. Though he had not the power to work with other men, he was a daring traveller, capable of assuming any disguise in order to secure knowledge at first hand. His *Pilgrimage to El-Medinah and Meccah* shows him to have possessed an intimate knowledge of Eastern life and an understanding of Eastern character such as has rarely been attained by a European.

George Borrow (1803—1881) had many of the characteristics of Burton. Both were bold fighters, famous linguists, men of sturdy bodies and eager restless souls. The gypsy nature characterised both, and both were most at home among the tramp classes of all countries. Borrow was a Protestant enthusiast whom the Bible Society chose to travel in Spain, carrying about their religious literature. This work pleased him, but when he came to write his report he forgot that he was writing for a missionary society, and wrote his well-known book *The Bible in Spain*. The Bible Society was probably both puzzled and perturbed, but Borrow has left behind in this bright and breezy volume the best book ever written by an Englishman about Spain. Like it, *Lavengro* and *The Romany Rye* are largely autobiographical. They show that even in nineteenth-century England a life as adventurous as the lives of mediæval romance could still be lived, and they embody an intimate knowledge of the wandering groups of gypsies which is unrivalled since, except by Mr Watts-Dunton's *Aylwin*.

§ 3. *Oscar Wilde*

We have reached the last figure of our period, and it is the most mournful. Oscar Wilde (1854—1900) was the son of distinguished parents, the bright boy of school and the brilliant student of his universities, Dublin and Oxford. He was the apostle of pleasure and artistic beauty. He says himself that he utterly rejected the doctrine of his mother's favourite quotation, those lines of Goethe translated by Carlyle:

> "Who never ate his bread in sorrow,
> Who never spent the midnight hours
> Weeping and waiting for the morrow,
> He knows you not, ye heavenly powers."

In early life Wilde was all compact of insincerity; he posed so much that he forgot how to be himself. He and his disciples paraded all sorts of follies; they flaunted peacocks' feathers, wore their hair long, and bedecked their bodies with velvet and jewels. Wilde's talk was flashing, his plays *Lady Windermere's Fan* and *The Importance of being Earnest* delighted the theatres with their smart epigrammatic dialogue, and his essays astonished people with their wit. Then in 1898 what seemed the end of all this brilliancy came. Wilde was sentenced to imprisonment with hard labour for two years. It was while eating this bread of sorrow that he thought his deepest thought and did his best work. *De Profundis* gives the history of his spirit during the terrible time. It and *A Ballad of Reading Gaol*, which was written after his release, overshadow all his other work. They are perhaps unique in literature, for no one else, gifted as Wilde was, ever had such an experience to describe. Such was the brilliant but tragic figure with which the Victorian era closed.

§ 1. *Landor and Minor Writers.*

Walter Savage Landor, 1775—1864.
Gebir, 1798.
Count Julian, 1812.
Imaginary Conversations, 1824—1853.
Pericles and Aspasia, 1836.
The Pentameron, 1837.
Andrea of Hungary, Giovanna of Naples, and Fra Rupert: A Trilogy, 1839—1841.
The Siege of Ancona, 1846.
Hellenics, 1847.
The Last Fruit off an Old Tree, 1853.
Heroic Idyls, 1863.
Mary Russell Mitford, 1786—1855.
Our Village, 1824—1832.
Recollections of a Literary Life, 1852.
Julius Hare, 1795—1855.
Guesses at Truth (with Augustus Hare, 1792—1834), 1827.
Arthur Helps, 1813—1875.
Friends in Council, 1847—1859.
Companions of My Solitude, 1851.
William Rathbone Greg, 1809—1881.
The Creed of Christendom, 1851.
Enigmas of Life, 1872.
William Brighty Rands, 1823—1882.
Henry Holbeach, Student in Life and Philosophy, 1865.
Verses and Opinions, 1866.
Chaucer's England, 1869.

§ 2. *Travel and Geography.*

F. L. McClintock, 1819—1907.
The Voyage of the Fox, 1859.
Amelia B. Edwards, 1831—1892.
A Thousand Miles up the Nile, 1877.

David Livingstone, 1813—1873.
Missionary Travels in South Africa, 1857.
Henry Morton Stanley, 1841—1904.
How I found Livingstone, 1872.
Through the Dark Continent, 1878.
In Darkest Africa, 1890.
John H. Speke, 1827—1864.
Journal of the Discovery of the Source of the Nile, 1863.
Richard Burton, 1821—1890.
A Pilgrimage to El-Medinah and Meccah, 1855.
George Borrow, 1803—1881.
The Zincali, 1841.
The Bible in Spain, 1843.
Lavengro, 1851.
The Romany Rye, 1857.
Wild Wales, 1862.

§ 3. *Oscar Wilde.*

Oscar Wilde, 1854—1900.
Poems, 1881.
Intentions, 1891.
Lady Windermere's Fan, 1892.
A Woman of no Importance, 1893.
The Importance of being Earnest, 1895.
A Ballad of Reading Gaol, 1898.
De Profundis, 1905.

INDEX

www.ingramcontent.com/pod-product-compliance
Ingram Content Group UK Ltd.
Pitfield, Milton Keynes, MK11 3LW, UK
UKHW042142280225
455719UK00001B/48